SCIENCE FOR SEXUAL HAPPINESS

SCIENCE FOR SEXUAL HAPPINESS

A GUIDE TO RECLAIMING EROTIC PLEASURE

BY CAFFYN JESSE

EROSPIRIT

The names and identifying details of clients have been changed to protect their anonymity.

Illustrations:

Figure drawings introducing chapters adapted from drawings in the Rijksmuseum's Rijksstudio Collection, except p. 62 which is from Wikimedia Commons (Egon Schiele - *Aktselbstbildnis* 1918)

For figures 4, 6, 7, 8, 9, 11 and 12, Caffyn Jesse worked with the artist S. Murali Shanmugam to create original illustrations.

Figures 1, 5, 10, 13 and 14 are drawn by Caffyn Jesse.

Figures 2 and 3, drawings of sympathetic and parasympathetic innervation, are by Blausen.com staff. "Blausen gallery 2014". Wikiversity Journal of Medicine. DOI:10.15347/wjm/2014.010. ISSN 20018762 and were changed by Caffyn Jesse to include the vulva. Creative commons licensing.

Figure 8, amygdala hijack drawing, uses a drawing by ManosHacker as a base. Creative commons licensing.

Mandala drawings, dog illustrations and the Joy Jar were adapted from drawings found on the Internet, using graphics subject to no known copyright restrictions.

Image of a human body in a pentagram from Heinrich Cornelius Agrippa's (1486 -1535) Libri tres de occulta philosophia.

Postures cartoon by Sacha Chua, creative commons licensing.

Mind map examples © Sophia Faria, used with permission.

Cover illustration by Franz Marc (*Broken Forms*).

Library and Archives Canada Cataloguing in Publication

Caffyn, Jesse, author

Science for Sexual Happiness: A Guide to Reclaiming Erotic Pleasure / Caffyn Jesse.

Includes bibliographical references and index. ISBN 978-0-9738332-3-2 (paperback)

1. Sex therapy. 2. Sex. 3. Psychic trauma--Patients-- Rehabilitation. I. Title.

RC557.C33 2016 613.9'6 C2016-906114-0

Designed by Mark Hand.

www.erospirit.ca

Contents

Acknowledgements

This book contains exercises used in the practice of somatic sex education, gathered and developed from many sources. My somatic sex education colleagues and students are ongoing and invaluable sources of ideas, learning and inspiration. I am so grateful to this community. Particular mentors and friends whose teachings are foundational for my practice include Mehdi Dervish, Dr. Elizabeth Ferguson, Dr. Ellen Heed, Dr. Joseph Kramer, Dr. Betty Martin, Christiane Pelmas, Elfi Emaya Dillon-Shaw, Dr. Liam 'Captain' Snowdon and Roy Turpin.

I am so grateful to friends and colleagues who read this book in manuscript and provided invaluable suggestions. A special thanks to Meredith Reynolds, my wonderful London, UK-based colleague, who devoted much time and expertise to helping me shape this book, and Sophia Faria, whose assistance has been invaluable. I am deeply appreciative of students and clients who read, worked on exercises and offered feedback.

I am thankful for Ruth M. Buczynski, PhD and the National Institute for the Clinical Application of Behavioral Medicine (NICABM). The NICABM programs on trauma and brain science, directed to clinical practice, are important background for my writing and my work. Reading books by Dr. Pat Ogden, founder of Sensorimotor Psychotherapy, Dr. Peter Levine, founder of Somatic Experiencing, and Dr. Bessel van der Kolk, a pioneer in treating and articulating the effects of trauma on the body, all had a profound impact on my work as a somatic sex educator. They are generous authors whose wisdom I hope I have integrated in my practice and my writing.

In 2015, I had the opportunity to study with Staci Haines at the STROZZI Institute, and experiencing somatic coaching there had a great impact on my understanding of the way autonomic nervous system reactions become embodied habits.

I am grateful to my friend Dr. Douglas Wahlsten, whom I relentlessly pepper with questions about neuroplasticity. Though this book was inspired in many ways by our connection, he has not reviewed it, and the mistakes are all mine.

Introduction

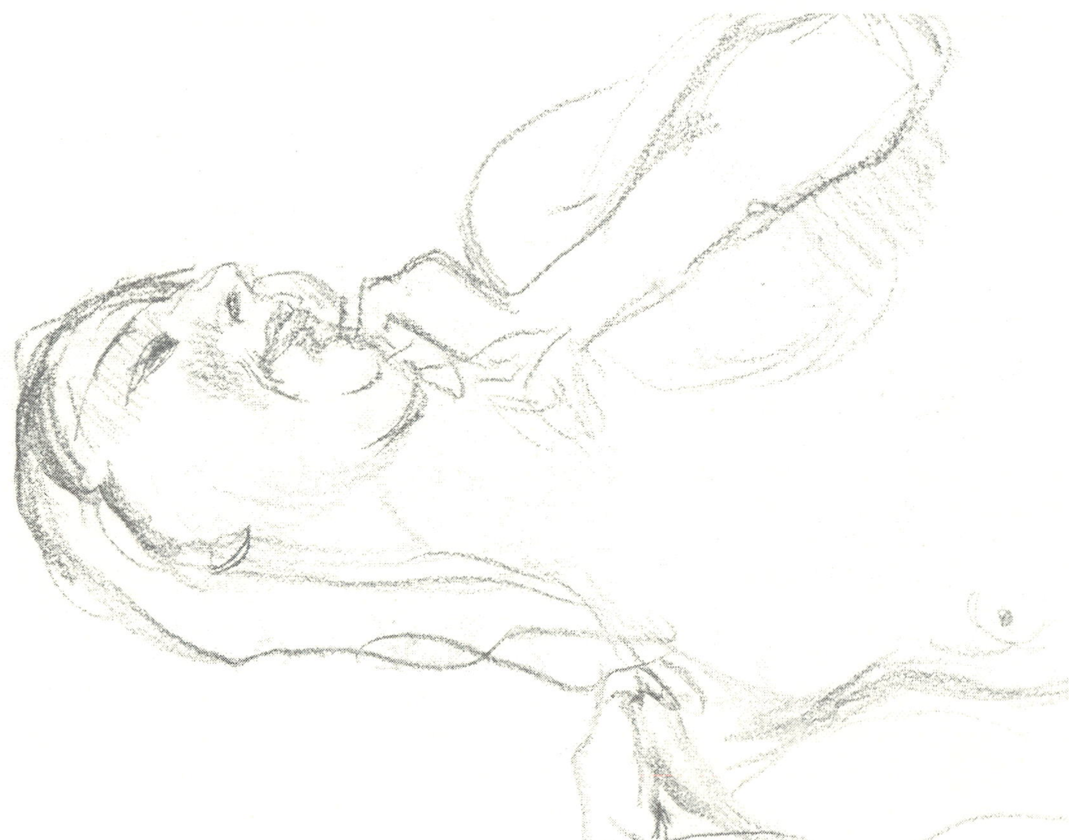

People come to work with me because they cannot access the fullness of erotic pleasure, alone or with a lover. Some say life seems safer and happier when they disconnect from sexual energy entirely, as sexual arousal or sexual relationships always bring a sense of dysregulation and distress. Some need the limerance of a new relationship to feel sexual, while others find their turn-ons only happen through dangerous liaisons. Others find they cannot access pleasure without the help of violent fantasies, pornography or compulsive behaviors that seem out of alignment with their heartfelt values. All these ways of being seem perfectly understandable when we know how sexual trauma and neglect impact the nervous system.

I often work with people who have engaged in years of talk therapy, and who have developed great insight into trauma and neglect they have experienced. But we can have all the insight in the world, and still feel paralyzed when it comes to experiencing joyful sex, asking for what we want sexually, and living our particular and ever-shifting sexual identities with confidence and peace. Somatic practices engage with our bodies' unconscious processes, so we can undo the effects of trauma and neglect at the cellular level.

There is such hope in knowing that just as our nervous systems change in response to trauma and neglect, so they will change in response to pleasure and play. The brain is not a physiologically static organ. It is continually changing, in response to the environment and what we pay attention to. It changes by our actions and our habitual thoughts. The whole nervous system is continually changing, learning and growing, or contracting and becoming inhibited. Just as muscles grow when we work out and atrophy when we do not, the brain and the nervous system grow and evolve with more enrichment and diverse stimulation. We can create new practices and form new habits, including the habit of sexual happiness. We can rewire our nervous systems with positive experiences of physical pleasure. We can repair damaged attachment systems with experiences of feeling cherished in our sexuality, and encouraged and prized for who we are as erotic beings.

The exercises I have gathered and developed here are for people who want to explore and reclaim their sexual wholeness. They are neural exercises that work in various ways to expand and integrate nervous system functions. 'Integration' is a key concept in the project of reclaiming erotic pleasure. We can wire bi-directional neural pathways that integrate body and brain. We can integrate sexual energy with our whole body and weave it through our lives. We can integrate heart, mind, voice and genitals. We can build integration within the brain, linking cortical structures with the limbic system and brainstem. We can integrate sexual expression with our heartfelt values. We can accept and integrate various aspects of our erotic selves. We can integrate our sexual history into a new story, where the past is teacher instead of a source of shame. We can integrate our unique individuality and sexual identity into the human community, and the world of nature and spirit.

Somatic practices empower us to regulate our nervous systems, so we have more sense of choice, and therefore safety, in our relationship with sex. Indeed, we can only really open to erotic pleasure when we have a foundational sense of safety. To trust ourselves and others, we also need to experience setting clear boundaries, and feel the power of asking for what we want and being listened to. As we feel more resourced, we gain in ability to stay present from moment-to-moment with erotic feeling, alone and with others. Through the actual *practice* of being in touch with our own courage and resilience, we can learn to choose pleasure, practice happiness, and bring more pleasure and happiness into our world.

A good first step in reclaiming erotic pleasure is cultivating a sense of celebration for all the ways erotic energy shows up in us. We can learn to welcome the feeling of sexual energy without judging it or needing to act on it. Erotic energy is life-force energy, sacred and innocent, powerful and magnificent. The exercises in this book help people learn to *play* with sexual energy—something so few of us have been encouraged to do. We can only expand into what is possible for us sexually when we can explore cultivating erotic feeling playfully, at a pace that is just right for us. With curiosity and without compulsion, we can practice noticing when and how we want to invite sex into our lives. As we learn to play with this energy, we can also learn to have more choice about how to access it, what to do with it, who to play with and how to play.

The work of healing and reclaiming erotic pleasure is playful. It is also profoundly important, to the evolution of each person's psyche, for our intimate and social relationships, and for the world.

Exercise 1: Mind maps of 'welcoming in' and 'letting go'

Can you imagine a way of being sexual that is energized and playful, passionate and flowing? What kind of environment would truly nourish you erotically? What is your deepest intention for this journey? How does that intention translate into everyday life? What are your specific goals? What resources can support you in meeting them?

Where has sexual dysfunction shown up in your life or your environment? What are you feeling a need to move away from?

A mind map is a graphic that uses words and images to represent ideas, tasks and associations that 'radiate' from a central question, image or idea. It is a way to engage both image and language functions of the brain in visioning and problem-solving. On the following pages you will find examples to inspire, plus space for mind maps on the theme of what you want to avoid or move away from, and what you want to move toward and embody. Draw five or more different-colored lines radiating from the central circle. Allow words, symbols, colors and images to begin populating your mind maps.

Use this process to feel into the vision that wants to be born. Keep working on and evolving these drawings as you go through the book.

Mind map examples
courtesy Sophia Faria

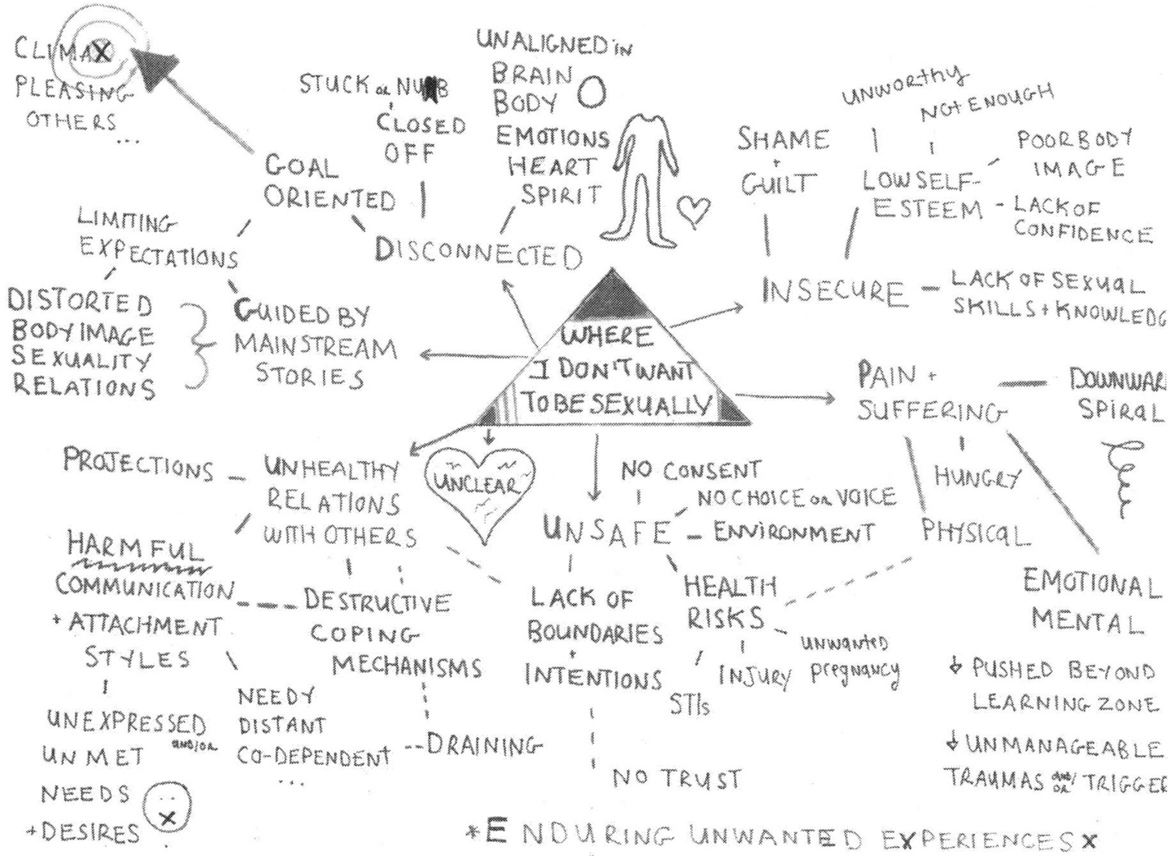

MY SEXUAL WHOLENESS
SPIRIT
EMOTIONS
MIND
HEART
BODY
BRAIN
ALIGNED
INTIMATE
CONNECTED
with ALL of LIFE
WILLINGNESS TO SURRENDER
UNION
SACRED
HONOURING
PRACTICE
PRAYERFUL
FOLLOW BLISS + JOY +
YES!
EROTIC ENERGY
ORGASMIC
PLEASUREFUL
JUICY
HONEY
PRESENCE
AWARENESS
CHOICE
FREE
FULL
EXPRESSION + COMMUNICATION
VOICE
HEALING
- ON ALL LEVELS
INDIVIDUAL
COLLECTI
SELF
LOVE + CARE
SENSUAL,
EMBODIMENT
SENSES
NATURE
ELEMENTS
TRANSFORMATIVE
JOYFUL
HUMAN
RELATIONS
DEEPLY
NOURISHING
BALANCED
RECIPROCAL
Clear
HEART,
INTENTIONS
BOUNDARIES +
CONTAINER
TIME, SPACE
AGREEMENTS
SAFE
EMOTIONAL
+
MENTAL
WELL EQUIPPED
TO NAVIGATE
CHALLENGES
HEALTHY RESPONSE TO
TRAUMAS
TRIGGERS
PHYSICAL
Sexually
healthy
CREATIVE
FLOW
Play
EXPLORATION
DISCOVERY
NO PRE-DETERMINED
DESTINATION
BREAT

Where I don't want to be sexually

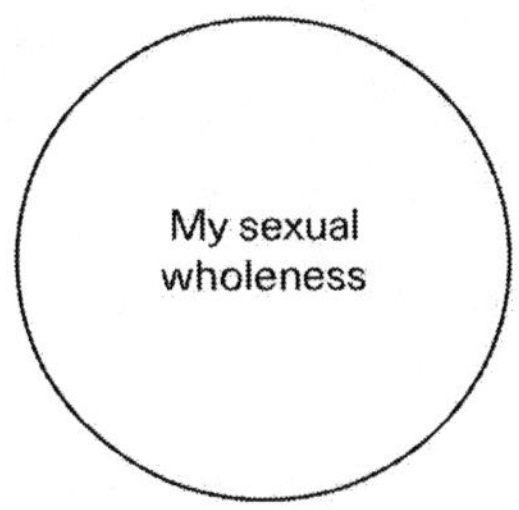
My sexual
wholeness

Figure 1: Self as *soma*

The Greek word *soma* means 'the living body,' 'the body-soul,' 'the living organism in its wholeness.' It is a better expression than we have in the English language for the fact that as human beings we are beings of mind, body, spirit and emotions. We are social and relational beings, and we are part of nature and the environment. We heal and reclaim erotic pleasure in relationships, connectedness, and context rather than as decontextualized people with body parts. We are complex, relational beings who can be hurt by personal and cultural forces. We are resilient and courageous. We can change.

We surround sex with trauma and neglect that separate mind from body, spirit and emotions. Our bodies are too distressed or dysregulated to feel fully. Spirit seems to abandon us. Our emotions are chaotic and unrecognized, so we disconnect from what we feel. Trauma and neglect also isolate us. If we are not cared for, kept safe, helped and cherished, we experience a sense of dis-integration, of not belonging. Reclaiming erotic pleasure involves establishing connections within the self, with others and community, with the world of nature and spirit, and with what makes life joyful.

As you proceed through these exercises, I invite you to give attention to the self as *soma*.

Trauma, Neglect and the Nervous System

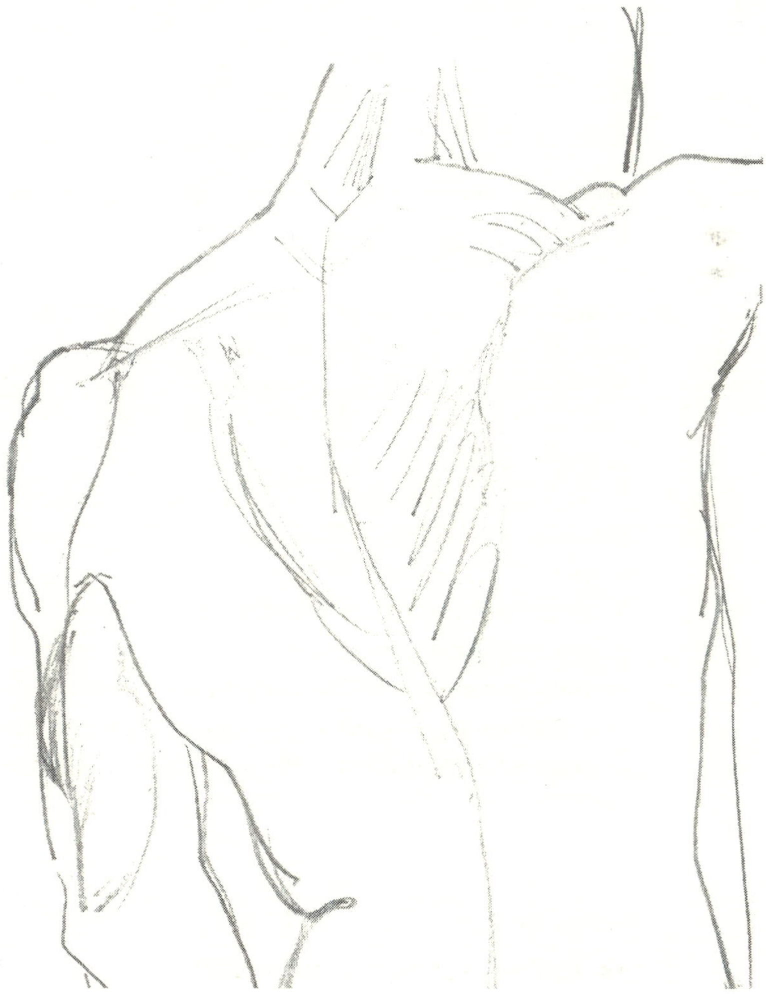

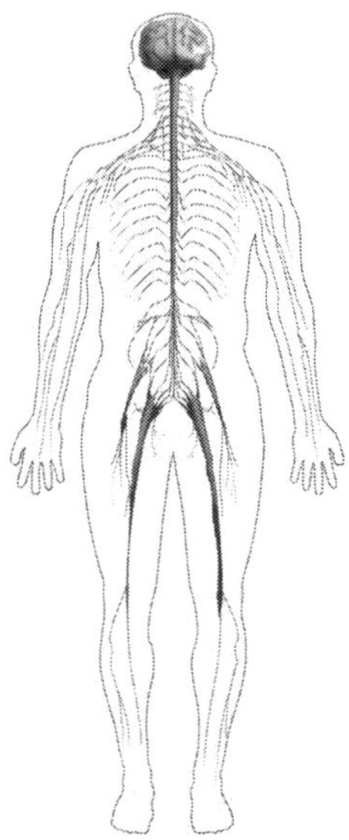

The shocking statistics on sexual assault, rape, child sexual abuse and partner violence show that sexual trauma is commonplace. Trauma can be chronic, with ongoing sexual exploitation that reoccurs over and over. This is often the case for the one in five children who are sexually abused before they turn 18 years old. Trauma is sometimes a single terrifying event of violence or assault. One in five women is raped. Trauma can also be subtle. Oppressions, micro-aggressions and chaotic life conditions result in lasting injury. Sexual violence is pervasive and it is also targeted. Trauma happens more frequently to women than to men, and more frequently to native women and women of color than to white women. Queer, gay, lesbian and bisexually-identified people are disproportionally subjected to sexual violence, and transgender people face even more danger. Living in a culture where sexual trauma is both commonplace and targeted affects us all.

In the past few decades a new scientific understanding has emerged of how trauma can lead to lifelong difficulties accessing sexual pleasure and navigating sexual relationships. As victims of trauma contend with their lived experience of terror and powerlessness, trauma can get stuck in the body. Years after a specific trauma ends, some survivors continue to embody nervous system responses evoked by deep distress. To gain awareness of how this happens, it is helpful to understand the basic structure of the autonomic nervous system.

THE NERVOUS SYSTEM

Awake or asleep, we are buzzing with billions of electrical and chemical messages traveling to and from the brain through the neurons and fibers of the nervous system. The **autonomic nervous system** controls processes that operate outside our conscious awareness. It monitors internal body conditions, and activates or inhibits the functions of cardiac muscle, smooth muscle and glands. The **sympathetic** branch controls the autonomic functions that happen when we are excited and alert. The **parasympathetic** branch controls the autonomic functions that happen when we are relaxed and at ease. Sympathetic and parasympathetic systems together regulate mood, along with the rate and force of breath and heartbeat, the relaxation or constriction of sphincters, and the accessibility of sexual arousal, erection and orgasm.

Stress manifests in physiological processes throughout the body. The sympathetic nervous system's 'fight or flight' response is triggered. We feel vigilant, anxious, and ready for action. The parasympathetic system returns the body to homeostasis after a stressful event. Parasympathetic hyperactivation associated with stress triggers nervous system hypoarousal. Blood pressure and heart rate drop through a 'vasovagal response.' We feel lightheaded, confused, and might even lose consciousness.

As we respond to the distress and nurturance of our lives, patterns of autonomic nervous system activation take shape in us. We develop default ways of meeting challenges and opportunities. Behavioral tendencies are embedded in our biological structure; we become the aliveness, agitation, distraction or presence that we practice.

When we want to welcome expanded erotic pleasure into our lives, we often need more than a set of instructions for how to have better sex. We need to find ways to become more calm, excited, attentive and alive; we need to make change in our autonomic nervous system function. Through somatic practices, we can open dialogue with our unconscious patterns and habitual reactions.

The autonomic nervous system reacts continually to input from other parts of the nervous system. **Sensory nerves** relay signals from skin, nose, mouth, eyes and ears, affecting our arousal or hyperarousal. As **motor nerves** convey commands from brain to striated muscles, movement, exercise and stillness affect the autonomic nervous system. The **enteric nervous system** is embedded in the lining of the gastrointestinal system and controls digestion. How we relate to our food tube has profound effects on our mood, and the vigilance of our autonomic nervous system affects digestion.

Brain-based learning and conscious thoughts have impact on unconscious physiological processes. Body-based exercises can change our minds, and changing our minds can affect stress reactivity throughout the body.

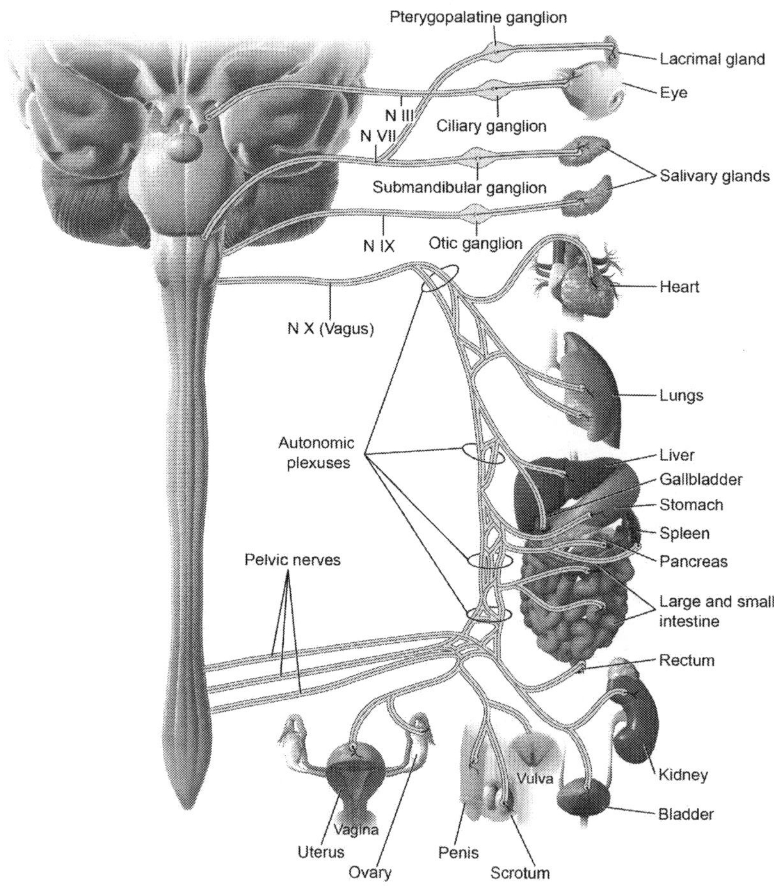

Figure 2: Parasympathetic innervation
drawing by Blausen.com staff, Blausen gallery 2014 with edits by Caffyn Jesse

Note that the vagus nerve exits the brainstem above the spinal cord and wanders through the body, innervating the organs of the abdomen and joining with pelvic nerves that innervate the genitals. The vagus nerve communicates with the facial cranial nerve, and the accessory nerve that innervates neck and shoulders. It controls the muscles of the larynx (speech).

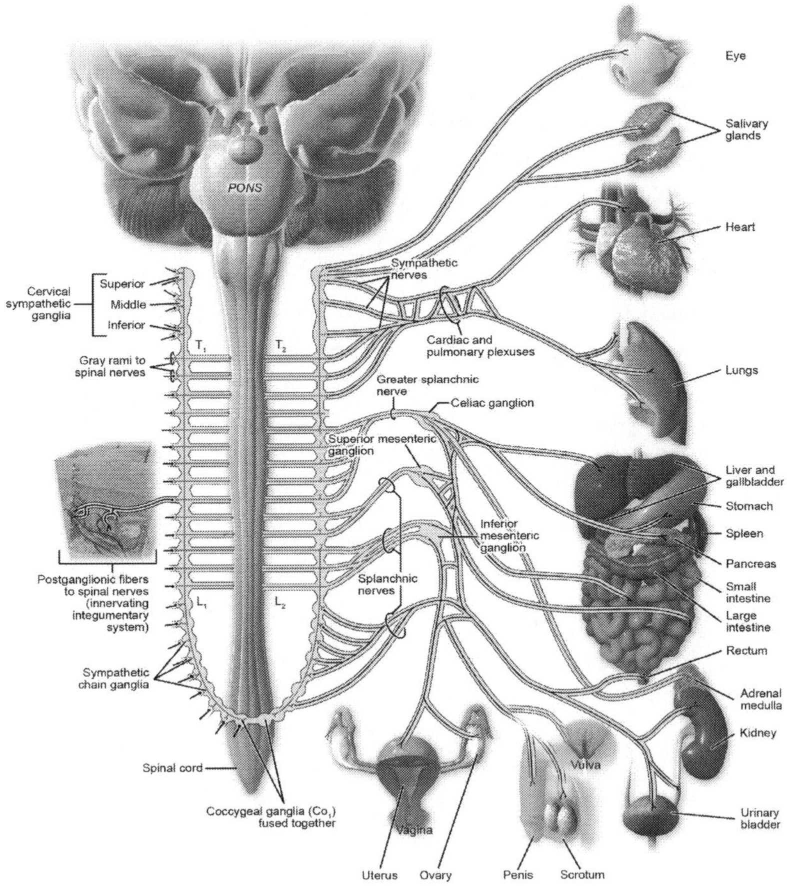

Figure 3: Sympathetic innervation
drawing by Blausen.com staff, Blausen gallery 2014 with edits by Caffyn Jesse

Fibers from the sympathetic nervous system also innervate almost every organ and system. Together with the parasympathetic nervous system, the sympathetic nervous system regulates things as diverse as pupil diameter and urinary output, as well as sexual function.

FIGHT, FLIGHT, APPEASE, FREEZE, DISSOCIATE

The sympathetic nervous system goes into hyperarousal when it is preparing us to face a threat. The amygdala in the brain senses danger before we can consciously evaluate a situation (see figure 8, Amygdala hijack). Powerful neurotransmitters and neurohormones, including cortisol and adrenaline, get released into our system before we ever consciously notice we are afraid. Our 'fight-or-flight' response is empowered so we can face or escape danger. When fight or flight seem impossible, we might find ourselves smiling despite our fear, and making gestures of surrender, as our 'appease' response is empowered. And when we cannot fight, flee or appease, but must endure extreme distress, we go into hypoarousal. We freeze, and then collapse, dissociate, go numb.

Fight, flight, appease, freeze and dissociate are wonderful, lifesaving autonomic nervous system responses to danger. They are problematic only if they get stuck in the body and become patterns deeply grooved into the nervous system. Then our unconsciously-regulated physiological states will limit our ability to live in alignment with our conscious choices. It can feel difficult or impossible to form intimate bonds and navigate passionate sexual relationships.

With the experience of trauma, the nervous system can become dysregulated. People can cycle between hypersensitivity and insensitivity, agitation and unaliveness. Nervous system dysregulation affects cardiovascular, respiratory, immune, digestive and reproductive function, along with memory, learning and relationships. Chronically high cortisol levels are found in the bloodstream. Upper-chest 'stress breathing' shuts down awareness, mobility and aliveness of the pelvic diaphragm. Neurochemical imbalances affect gut health and mental health. The legacy of trauma shows up in a huge variety of physical symptoms, including autoimmune disease, pelvic pain, and mysterious ailments in the digestive tract and reproductive system. Sexual arousal may be inaccessible or feel compulsive. The physiology of trauma also manifests emotionally. People often feel upset and angry, or withdrawn and numb, without knowing why.

The physiological and psychological effects of neglect are also profound. Experiments in psychobiology and neuroscience have consistently found that neglect has a dysregulating effect on the nervous system. Over fifty years ago, Harry Harlow's experiments with infant monkeys deprived of maternal care showed how the *absence* of touch can lead to death. More recent studies have drilled down into the complex biomolecular operations through which neglect exerts its intense effects. The Canadian lab of Michael Meaney demonstrated how a lower incidence of anal-genital licking by a mother rat leads to changes in the gene expression of infants in her care, affecting their stress reactivity throughout life, and potentially having impacts on future generations. In human studies, emotional neglect in childhood is associated with increased stress hormone concentrations in adults. Digestion, sexual behavior, social competence, memory and learning are among the many systems affected by neglect. Neglected people often lack motivation, excitement and pleasure, including the pleasure of connecting with others and themselves erotically.

When we are feeling resourced and resilient, we can shift from vigilance and agitation to become calm and relaxed, with a positive imagination of the future. But when we are dealing with unresolved 'stuck' trauma or neglect, we live in a chronic state of physiological stress, sensing danger everywhere. Years after a specific trauma ends, although in situations we consciously judge as safe, our autonomic nervous system is hyper-alert. Perhaps sleep is disturbed, sexual response is flat, bowels don't work, touch makes us want to scream. We may struggle with an uncontrollable sense of shame or blame, intrusive thoughts, or feelings of being anxious, angry, irritated or agitated. Some people get stuck in hypoarousal, and feel shut down, frozen, spaced out, sluggish and disconnected. Often people cycle between states of feeling overstressed and unalive, within an hour or within a lifetime. When stuck in hyperarousal, it can feel impossible to tolerate the excitement that comes with sex. When stuck in hypoarousal, we need danger, drama, or hyperstimulation to arouse the nervous system and feel sexual.

Understanding how the nervous system works is important for releasing shame. This is new information I so wish I had as a young person recovering from trauma. I thought there was something irrevocably wrong with me, that I was screwed-up and unworthy. I thought I 'should' be able to enjoy sexual pleasure and access arousal readily. I didn't understand my emotional upheavals, or why my sexual aliveness arrived in unwanted and obsessive forms. I had impaired connection with mind, body, spirit and emotions. I listened to the voices in my head. Various talk therapies did little to shift my sense of wellbeing or help me build capacity for joyful sexuality. When I discovered somatic sex education, I was able to work through body-based exercises and experiences to create change. With a lived understanding of unconscious nervous system function, I can hold the confused younger woman I was in compassion and loving kindness. I can coach clients to do this for themselves.

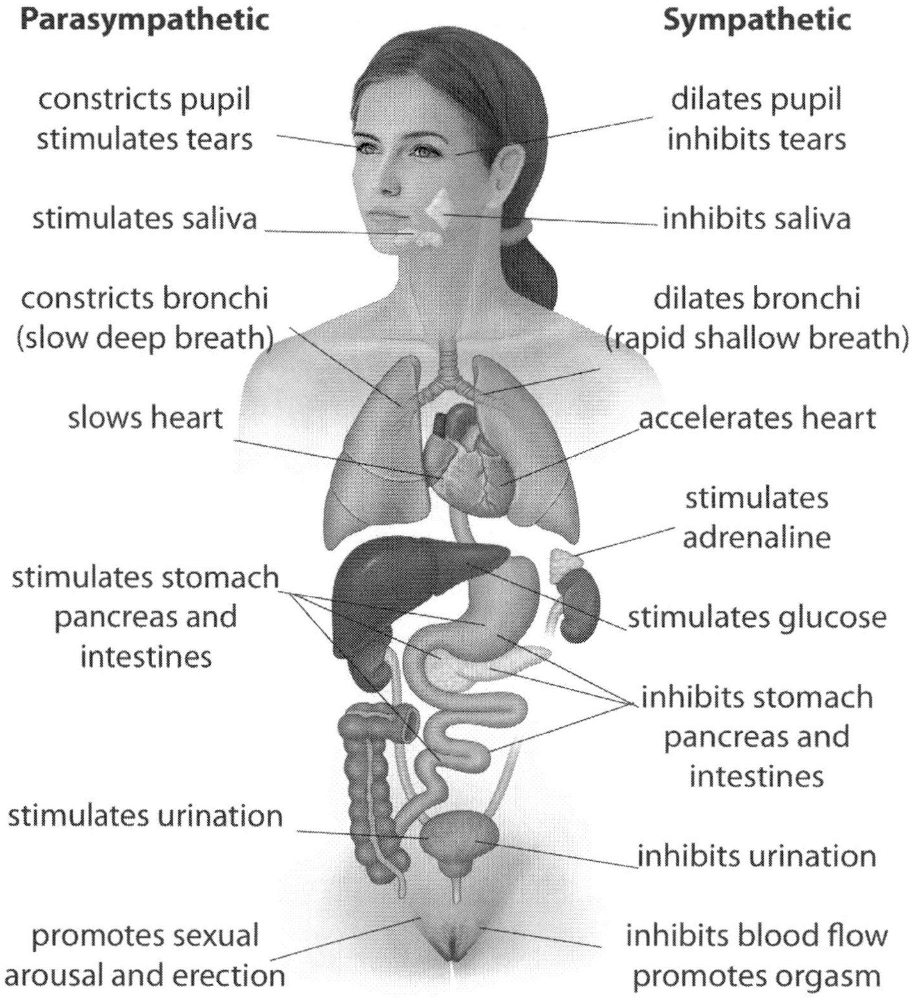

Figure 4: Parasympathetic and sympathetic nervous systems

Sexual trauma and neglect are individual and collective experiences. We experience specific traumas that affect us profoundly. And we are living amidst institutional standards, family systems and normative practices that perpetuate sexual violence, segregation and domination. A host of macro and micro-aggressions punish sexual identities and experiences outside a norm that almost no one fits inside. Neglect of our sexuality is also vigorously enforced. Most children are born into a world that disregards their sexuality and admonishes or exploits its expression. Adults typically have their sexual experiences rationed to occasional and unsatisfying exchanges. It is well past time we recognize that this neglect in itself is traumatizing. By working and playing to transform our personal neurobiology, we also look to understand and transform the social context.

Self-Regulation and the Learning Zone

Reclaiming erotic pleasure in the wake of trauma and neglect means being able to bring awareness to how autonomic nervous system responses feel in our bodies, and where and when they appear in ways that serve us. Specific physical practices empower us to regulate the nervous system when we want more choice.

When we are excited, the sympathetic branch of our autonomic nervous system is dominant. Heartbeat increases, blood flows into striated muscles, focus narrows to the present moment. We feel stimulated and alive to sensation and the world around us. When we are relaxed, the parasympathetic branch of the autonomic nervous system is dominant. We feel content, calm and peaceful. Heartbeat slows, focus broadens. We breathe deeply, savour and rest. Under normal conditions our bodies swing back and forth between sympathetic and parasympathetic dominance all day long. You might have noticed that you feel more awake and active in the morning, and dreamy and relaxed after lunch, or you might have a different pattern. There is even an alteration between sympathetic and parasympathetic dominance with every breath. Each time we breath in, our heart rate increases slightly as our 'awake and take' aliveness is activated. Each time we breathe out, our heart rate slows as our 'rest and digest' relaxation is activated. This gentle and complex flow between sympathetic and parasympathetic dominance changes when we are preparing to face a threat, and the 'fight, flight, appease, freeze and dissociate' responses are activated through sympathetic hyperarousal and parasympathetic hypoarousal.

READ THIS FIRST!
Finding the sweet spot: working in your personal learning zone

Learning to regulate autonomic nervous system responses and reclaim erotic pleasure may at times feel stressful, even scary. And we can learn to recognize the difference between feeling uncomfortable and feeling unsafe. We can learn to regulate and tolerate the stress mobilization of discomfort and gradually restore a sense of safety and aliveness to the whole body. But only when we work in our personal 'learning zone.' That means not too much, and not too fast. For each person the learning zone will be different. ***Many of the exercises in this book will not be suitable or relevant for some people.***

It is a biological principle (*hormesis*) that exposure to just-enough stress creates benefits, even though exposure to any more stress is harmful. We each can get familiar with that feeling of just-enough stress within ourselves. For learning, we need just-enough stress to create a manageable challenge, and that just-right stress will be very different for each person. With too much stress, the autonomic nervous system will mobilize as hyperarousal or shut down in a frozen hypoaroused state. Pushing ourselves too hard can be painful and retraumatizing. With too little stress, we will stay stuck in our habits and experience nervous system atrophy. For each of us, it is important to continually assess the limits of our personal 'learning zone,' where we may be uncomfortable, but not unsafe. We can aim to work carefully within these limits, while challenging ourselves to continually expand them.

Before and during any exercise, keep checking in with yourself. Do you need more safety and holding in this moment, or more challenge? Do you need to expand your capacity for excitement, engagement and aliveness? Or would it be better to work on building up your capacity for relaxation and detachment? *Go as slowly as you need to go, and keep tracking your feelings from moment-to-moment.* If you find you've gone too far or too fast, get the support you need to come back into your personal learning zone.

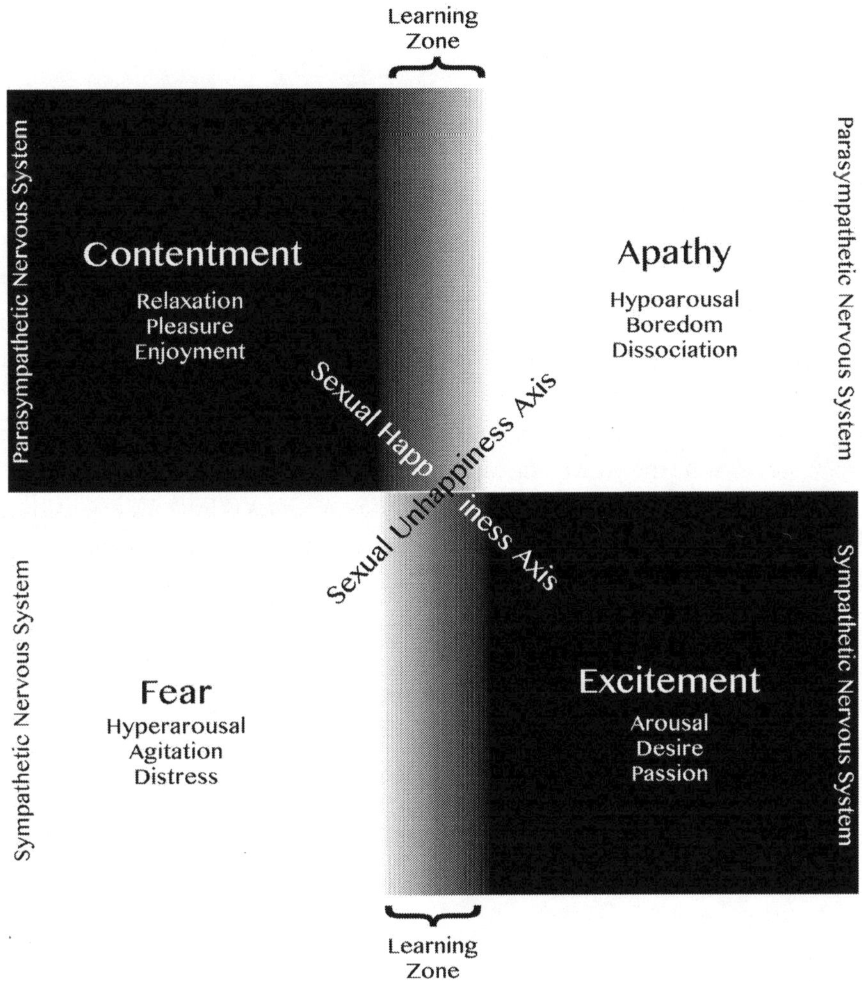

Figure 5: Finding the sweet spot: working in your personal learning zone

Sexual happiness involves both excitement and contentment.

Excited arousal is the domain of our sympathetic nervous system. If we feel under-resourced and unsafe, excitement can readily slip over into fear. We can learn to savor more excitement, challenging ourselves to feel more passion without slipping over into distress and anxiety (expanding capacity of the sympathetic nervous system).

Contented pleasure is the domain of our parasympathetic nervous system. If we are chronically agitated or dissociated, relaxed savoring can feel disengaging and dull. We can learn to feel more contentment, challenging ourselves to feel peaceful enjoyment without slipping over into apathy (expanding capacity of the parasympathetic nervous system).

Along the 'Sexual Happiness Axis,' as in all things, we only learn in our personal learning zone. This is the zone where we are challenged – and perhaps uncomfortable – without being unsafe.

DOGGIE WISDOM: AUTONOMIC NERVOUS SYSTEM HABITS

Think of dogs and how they express fear, stress, distress and anxiety. Different dogs have different fear responses. The same dog may have different stress responses to different situations. Some dogs are fighters. They bark loudly or growl. They try to make themselves look as large and threatening as possible, with a stiff, upright body, and hard and unblinking eyes. Their fur stands on end. If deeply stressed, they bite (Fight). Other dogs are timid. They run away, or cower to make themselves look small (Flight). Other dogs habitually want to please. They roll on their backs to show they aren't a threat, lick nervously, or cautiously wag their tail (Appease). Or they might stand very still, looking scared, with eyes wide, showing the whites, or avoiding eye contact (Freeze). If a dog has to endure a terrible situation, it goes limp, shuts down and collapses (Dissociate).

The reactions an anxious dog has are the same ones that we have. And just like dogs, we all have different temperaments and experiences, and different habitual autonomic nervous system reactions.

Exercise 2: Habits under stress

This exercise is about identifying your habitual reactions so you can be more aware of how you tend to react to stress. With awareness comes more choice.

Reflect on the different autonomic nervous system reactions listed. Identify times when you have felt this way, and the emotions you experienced when you were in this mode of responding to anxieties. Identify the autonomic nervous system reactions that are habitual for you, and ones you are less likely to practice. Then try on different doggie-inspired postures and gestures, like strange new sets of clothes. Role-play different defenses, or simply imagine doing so, working in your personal learning zone.

Autonomic Nervous System Defense	Describe your memories and feelings
FIGHT: hackles raised, teeth bared, bite, get big, low growl, get critical, get angry, push away, attack, hit, scream	
FLIGHT: Run away, back away, escape, hide, shrink, get small	
APPEASE: (dog) expose vulnerable belly (human) expose jugular vein by cocking head. Whine, cry for help, seek touch, cling, be nice, worried face, quiet high voice, grin	
FREEZE: unmoving, hyper-alert, stiff, paralyzed, tail tucked in /pelvic clench	
DISSOCIATE: go numb, go limp, collapse, become apathetic, play dead, fall silent, 'leave' mentally and emotionally without leaving physically.	

Think of dogs and how they express feeling good. If they are excited, their tails wag. They might act playful and bark, and run around tossing toys into the air. Humans are not so different. Dogs and humans express excited good feelings with their bodies, faces and sounds when they are joyful, delighted, enthusiastic, happy, thrilled, triumphant, confident, curious. It looks quite different when dogs are expressing relaxed good feelings. They might stretch and roll onto their backs. Their faces become soft and open. Humans too. We release the tension in our bodies when we are feeling contentment. Our pelvic muscles unclench and our postures change. Humans and dogs embody relaxed good feelings when we feeling safe, calm, loving, peaceful, satisfied, tender

Just as we can groove habitual autonomic nervous system reactions to hyperarousal and distress, we also can get habitual about how we either calm or stimulate our nervous system to feel good. Some people always seek excitement. They take risks, and have great adventures, but miss the joys of relaxed good feelings. Others habitually find their happiness in relaxation. They might be content with a quiet life, but miss the joys of challenge and excitement. Wherever we begin, we can expand our capacity to savour relaxed contentment through the parasympathetic nervous system and excited arousal through the sympathetic nervous system by working and playing in our personal learning zones.

Exercise 3: Habits of happiness

Filling in the following worksheet can help you gain awareness of how you feel when things are flowing. Notice the memories, people, places and animals that you feel good with. Notice the different dimensions of feeling good. Notice how feeling good affects your breath, posture, facial expression, heartbeat, and sensation on your skin. Notice any movement impulse. Do you want to dance and play, or lie down and stretch?

Describe feeling good write down specific memories, and describe people you feel good with	**Describe your excited or relaxed emotions**	**Describe your body feelings and postures**

Exercises 4–10: PORTALS

When we sense danger, there are many instantaneous physical effects. Some of these same effects can be replicated consciously. *Effects that happen unconsciously, yet can be controlled by the conscious mind, are portals to the autonomic nervous system. Through them, we can open dialogue between conscious and unconscious processes.*

P is for pelvic floor. Squeeze and release the muscles of the pelvic floor. Squeeze again, and release, focusing separately on anus, urethra, and vagina/penis.

O is for open. Close and open your eyes.

R is for reduced breath. Breathe slowly, breathe less.

T is for toes. Wiggle toes and fingers. Shake hands and feet.

A is for aaaahhh. Scrunch up your face, open your mouth, and say aaaahhh.

L is for Look and Listen. Name five specific things in your environment. Name five specific sounds in the world around you.

S is for saliva. Make water inside your mouth.

Pelvic floor

With any increase in anxiety, we immediately and unconsciously brace for action. The pelvic floor is the core structure involved in this process. We have all seen dogs raise their tails high and wave them when excited. And we've seen them pulling their tails between their legs, indicating fearful, self-protective surrender. Humans do something very similar with their pelvic floor muscles, despite the absence of a visible tail. If we are chronically hypervigilant, there will be one kind of pelvic floor activation. If we feel defeated, withdrawn or ashamed, there is another kind of pelvic floor activation. Both involve the unconscious clenching of pelvic floor muscles. When unresolved trauma gets stuck, we are likely to have a chronically clenched pelvic floor.

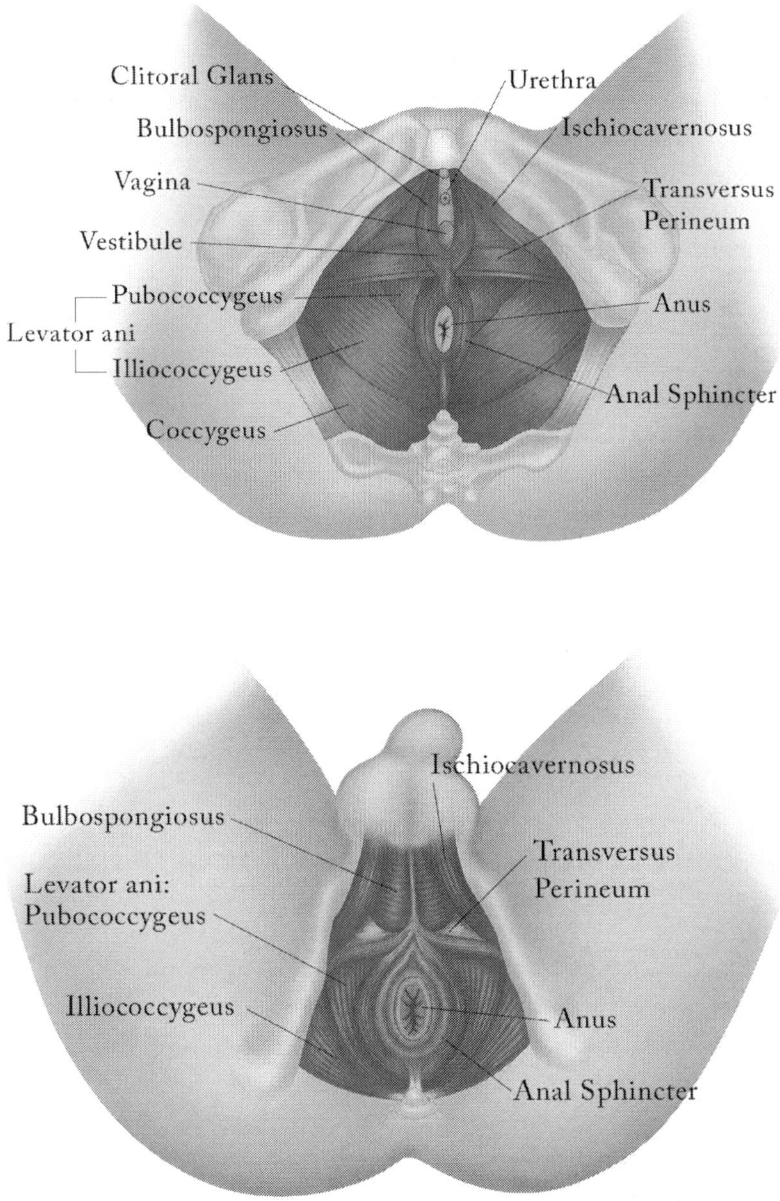

Figure 6: Pelvic floor muscles

A conscious, deliberate clench and release brings our awareness to the pelvic floor. We say to the autonomic nervous system, 'Thank you. I notice pelvic floor muscle activation is important. I can choose to clench, and I can choose to release my pelvic floor muscles when the time is right.'

Focusing separately on the muscles of the anus, urethra and vagina/penis is a more challenging practice that can add additional dimensions to this noticing. You may not be able to feel these muscles separately, especially at first, but it works just as well to simply imagine these structures, and imagine activating the muscles you would use to stop yourself from pooing or peeing.

Be sure to take time to notice the conscious release and relief you feel after letting the clench go. For some people, full release and relaxation doesn't feel possible, and conscious clenching only adds more tension to their chronic clench. Don't worry! Just do this exercise a little differently. Instead of clenching the pelvic floor, enhance your awareness by simply noticing or imagining your deep breath going right down into the pelvic floor. Imagine your breath massaging your pelvic floor from the inside. Send loving gratitude to the protective clench.

Opening and closing the eyes

The pupils of our eyes expand in the dark and behind closed eyelids; they constrict in the light and when eyelids are open. Pupils respond to more than changes in light. They also respond to mental challenge, emotional turmoil and sexual arousal. Stimulation of the autonomic nervous system's 'awake and take' sympathetic branch prompts expansion of the pupils. When a problem is difficult, when you feel stressed, or you feel excited by sexual arousal, pupil size increases. Stimulation of the 'rest and digest' parasympathetic nervous system produces constriction. Eyelids usually blink unconsciously, and often blink more rapidly in response to stress. So deliberately opening and closing your eyes can open a portal between conscious and unconscious responses, and reassure the autonomic nervous system.

Reduced breath

Breathing shallowly and quickly is a life-saving autonomic nervous system response to danger. If we live in a chronic state of emergency, we likely have a chronic pattern of 'stress breath.' This means we are overbreathing, causing CO_2 levels in the blood to decrease. With this imbalance, oxygen is bound more tightly to hemoglobin in the blood, and not released to the tissues as readily. The heart has to work harder to move less-oxygenated blood around the body. Blood pressure is elevated. The body's pH becomes more acidic. A vicious circle is established: anxiety leads to rapid breathing, while the consequent biochemical imbalance triggers biophysical anxiety, exacerbating nervous system distress. There are unnecessary demands on other systems and organs including the kidneys, the liver and the skin. Feelings of fatigue, disquiet and distraction become ordinary.

We can intervene and create positive change in this cycle simply by consciously slowing down our breath.

Breathe out, and wait without breathing until you feel the body's authentic need for breath. Take a few regular breaths, then hold your in-breath until you feel an authentic need to let it go.

As a separate practice for reduced breath, breathe out, pause and then breathe in as slowly as you can, imagining you are breathing in through your skin. Take a few regular breaths. Breathe in, pause and then breathe out as slowly as you can, imagining you are breathing out through your skin.

Repeat your reduced breathing several times, and throughout the day.

Relax into an awareness that you will breathe as much as you need to, and maybe you don't need to breathe quite so much.

Toes and fingers, hands and feet

When we sense danger and the sympathetic nervous system goes into hyperarousal, adrenaline gives the body a tremendous amount of energy. When that energy goes unused it leads to physical agitation that often shows up as restless movement in the hands and feet. Consciously and deliberately expressing physical energy by clenching, shaking and wiggling your extremities can calm autonomic nervous system agitation. And if the physiology is in hypoarousal, frozen and numb, then conscious movement of the extremities can be enlivening. By moving toes, fingers, hands and feet, you are assuring unconscious systems that movement is still possible. You tell your soma, 'You're okay. You can get out of here if you need to.'

A is for aaaahhh. Scrunch up you face, open your mouth, and say aaaahhh.

The vagus nerve, primary nerve of the parasympathetic nervous system, is linked to nerves that regulate the striated muscles of the face. Facial muscles communicate visceral feelings. Brows furrow, lips purse, noses wrinkle, as these muscles describe inner feelings without our conscious awareness. When people are deeply stressed, their facial muscle tone goes flat. The vagus nerve is also linked to vocalization. Speaking and being spoken to in a reassuring, caring way is essential for creating a felt sense of safety. People lose the capacity to communicate—even to think—when they are pushing themselves or getting pushed beyond their learning zone. They cannot ask for what they need; their voice goes flat. People who suffer from chronic autonomic nervous system distress often have an unexpressive tone of voice and little facial expressivity.

But facial expressivity and tone of voice can also be played with consciously. It's fun! Open your mouth and say aaahhh. How many emotions can you express with this one syllable? Scrunch up your face, play with facial expressions, and play in the mirror as you might play with a baby. At first it might feel hard, silly or too vulnerable. But see if you can stretch yourself, to exercise and increase your vagal tone.

L is for look and listen: name five specific things and five specific sounds in the world around you.

Trauma and neglect can leave us literally disoriented. Continually bombarded by the physical and emotional symptoms of a hyperactivated nervous system, the body feels unsafe and we dissociate. It is hard to pay attention to our surroundings when we are distracted and unfocused, or stuck listening to the voices in our heads. Racing thoughts, being absorbed in catastrophic thoughts, or feeling caught up in negative evaluations of ourselves or the world around us are all part of the neural legacy of trauma and neglect.

By really looking at and listening to the immediate world around us, we can get oriented, feel safer, and come home to the present moment. To look for five specific things in our immediate environment, we need to feel safe enough to tune in.

Hypersensitivity to sound is a common way that trauma gets embedded in the nervous system. Noise may spark irritation, startle, or trigger a panicky feeling. So people learn to shut down sensation, stop listening for auditory cues, and cease appreciating the diversity of sounds in the environment.

Stop for a moment and really listen. Come into presence with the world around you. Let the voices in your head go quiet. Notice and name five specific sounds to reassure your autonomic nervous system that you are calm enough to do this.

S is for saliva. Make water inside your mouth

Dry mouth is a common symptom of stress. The autonomic nervous system, sensing danger, stops automatically producing the miraculous fluid saliva with its diverse healing properties. But usually, even when stressed, we can consciously make saliva flow just by paying attention to the inside of our mouth, and using a sucking action to bring water into it. This is a way of saying physically to the autonomic nervous system 'You can relax now.'

Exercise 11: Breath

We can consciously change our autonomic nervous system responses with our breath. When we are relaxed, our breathing slows and becomes deeper. By choosing to breath more slowly and deeply, we can relax. When feeling apathetic or unfocused, we can choose to increase our engagement and arousal simply by speeding up our breath.

Exercise 12: Posture

Play with your posture. We all have habitual postures. Some people are habitually hunched, with a tucked-in tail, protective of the heart and genitals. Some people lead with the chest, tail held high. Play with your posture and pay attention to what happens inside. Notice any emotional shifts that happen when you exaggerate the position of your shoulders and hips, or the way you hold your head.

What are the body sensations? Do images or words come up? What is your body habitually saying with posture? Can you play with saying something else?

'Play with Posture' drawing by Sacha Chua

Exercise 13: Slapping

Trauma and neglect can leave us feeling chronically unsafe inside our skin. We may become insensitive to touch, or hypersensitive to touch, or avoid situations where we might be touched.

With mindful self-slapping, we take an action and sensation that is often linked to memories of punishment and violence, and use it to help us better inhabit our own skin. We can increase sensate focus, enjoy a feeling of aliveness, and foster present moment awareness by slapping. Skin is the largest organ of the body, the place of boundary transition between self and not-self. By varying pressure, speed and vibration, we awaken the various kinds of touch-sensing nerves in our skin.

Try slapping or tapping on one side only: foot and ankle, calf and shin, and then move up your leg and slap your thigh. Slap for a minute, then stop and feel into the tingling sensations on the slapped side. Compare with the unslapped side.

How much slapping actually helps us feel fully awake and alive, without pushing us over the edge of our learning zone into a distressed response? For some people, gentle percussive taps are just-right. For others, vigorous spanking is just-right. Feel into your edges with this practice.

As another version of this practice, try slapping your bottom, and later your genitals. For a more challenging version of this practice, try it with a partner.

Variation: Slap for a minute and then close your eyes, tuning into the sensation in your skin. Say aloud, 'This is my body, this is my boundary. This is my body and nobody else's.'

Variation 2: Try tapping instead.

Exercise 14: Get activated

Practice feeling the activation of your nervous system as a high-intensity experience that is enlivening instead of frightening. When our nervous system is stuck on high alert, we often avoid experiences that are new, challenging, fearful and forceful. Try to imagine a simple, accessible activity that can help you feel your sympathetic nervous system activation in a safe and controlled way. What about going into a sex toy store, or attending a talk about sex? You might try watching a sexy movie, or taking a class in erotic arts. If this feels like way too much, you could try winking at someone, or looking at yourself in a sexually charged way. Pick the level of autonomic nervous system arousal that is right for you. You can activate your nervous system by imagining an activity or actually doing an activity. Try both!

Get your sympathetic nervous system activated, and notice how it feels to have your heart pounding, breath speed up, and pelvic floor clench, as you feel the fear, and do it anyway (or imagine doing it anyway). Be sure you stay in your learning zone, so you feel vital and challenged, but not truly unsafe.

Reflect on the idea of controlled risk-taking and how it fits or doesn't fit with the goals and intentions you have for your journey to sexual wholeness.

When trauma is stuck in the physiology, it can only be unstuck by exercises that engage and rewire neural systems, gradually building our capacity to regulate our physiological state. With patient practice, we will find we are no longer run by embedded trauma. Instead of fear, shame, stress, arousal, distress and indifference being feelings that happen or never happen *to* us, we can work with our nervous system to invite feelings that serve us better in different situations. By learning to self-regulate the autonomic nervous system, we can more easily choose to live in harmony with our values, and with the possibility of unfolding erotic joy.

Creating Safe Zones and Places of Refuge

A friendly hug, a doctor visit, an office party—present-day situations that are ostensibly safe may not feel safe at all for a trauma survivor. We can react physiologically as we did in a terrifying situation decades prior. Default fight, flight, appease, freeze or dissociate patterns are deeply grooved into our nervous system by personal and social histories. Recognizing these patterns is key to change, but it is not easy or simple to do this. Our ability to be aware of body sensations and emotions is compromised when the body is awash with stress hormones. To know our own physiology, we need to feel safe enough to tune in.

A woman in her thirties, Mary, came to see me because she yearned for an erotic connection with others, but she knew that her childhood had left her with wounds she didn't want to bring to a new relationship. From the age of six until she finally escaped to live on her own at sixteen, she had been brutally assaulted by a series of her mother's drunken boyfriends. She had never experienced a consensual sexual exchange. Mary said she was eager to experience a bodywork session, but her body told me she was afraid by making small, agitated movements. She had very little facial expressivity, and her gaze stayed downcast as she avoided my eyes. Mary and I spent several sessions focusing on exercises that would help her access a sense of grounded safety.

We want erotic freedom; we think we 'should' be able to enjoy sex. And we can try to override our physiology with conscious decisions to have sexual experiences. But during, or after, we are likely to find the person we picked to explore with is a jerk (Fight). We feel 'Let me out of here!' or 'I never want to see them again!' (Flight). Perhaps we lose control of the experiment and wind up agreeing to things we wish we hadn't. We get focused on giving them what they want (Appease). We can't ask for what we need; it's like we've lost our voice (Freeze). Or we find ourselves tuning out. In the middle of an erotic experience, we start thinking about tidying up the kitchen (Dissociate).

Making a cognitive decision to be sexual that is not interwoven with body, spirit and emotion leaves us vulnerable to falling into old patterns and creating new layers of trauma. When we can ground decisions in an integrated somatic awareness, we have a basis for creating real differences in how we act, react, and relate with ourselves and each other as erotic beings. Simply telling the mind to pay attention to the body is not enough. Body awareness may be inaccessible, as the mind keeps skittering away from the challenge. Getting mired in body awareness is another risk. People can feel destabilized by intrusive awareness of body sensation. To consciously integrate mind and body, we need a sense of grounded safety. We need a felt sense of our inner and outer resources, a supportive environment, and a reservoir of patience and compassion for ourselves.

The exercises in this section help us know somatically that we are resourced, and we have choices. To access a sense of grounded safety, we need to bring new awareness to resources we already have, and also to engage in real resource-building in the world. We can gradually learn to find a physiologically safe and stable home in our own bodies with a repertoire of self-care and self-regulation practices. As we deliberately foster an internal sense of safety, we can also make safer spaces in our outer world. When challenges get unmanageable, we need to know how to access places of refuge, without and within. We can engage in erotic experimentation fruitfully when we *embody* the deep knowledge we have choices.

GROUNDING AND CENTERING

Trauma 'upsets' us. We get off-balance, lose our ground. Centering and grounding, we reestablish connection with a felt sense of how we are held by gravity, by earth. We find again our own personal center of gravity, in the pelvis—the place where action and feeling originate, and where power resides. *Grounding and centering exercises help to create a feeling that we cannot be knocked off-balance by emotions, sensations or thoughts.*

Exercise 15: Centering

with thanks to STROZZI institute teachings, Richard Strozzi Heckler and Staci Haines, and Elfi Emaya Dillon Shaw

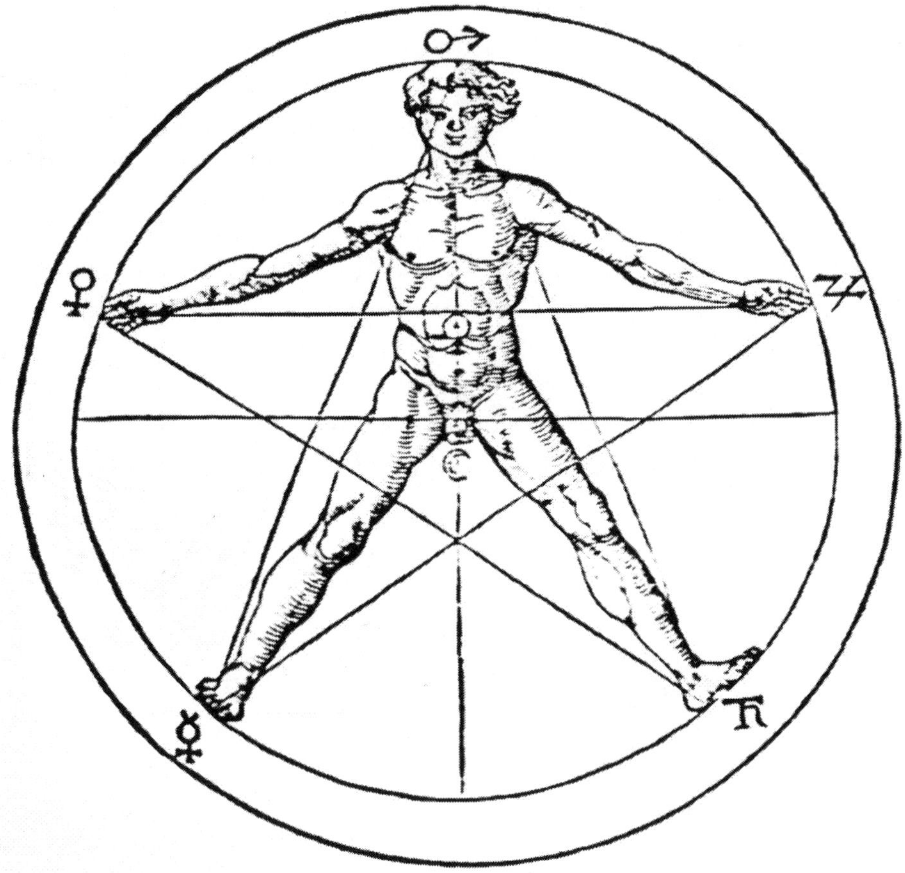

Relax and breathe into your pelvis. Shake your arms and hands. Let the shake travel all the way through your body as you shake off all your worries, discomforts and doubts. Shake until you have shaken it all off, and then let yourself come to stillness in the present moment.

Tune into the centerline of your body, running from your perineum (between genitals and anus) up to the top of your head. Relax your body around this centerline. Let the bones of your pelvis expand outward as you breathe into your pelvic diaphragm. Feel the pelvic diaphragm soften and expand. Relax your belly, feel your soft belly swell with your breath. Feel the unwinding of your digestive tract. Soften your heart. Release the restriction in your throat and jaw, release the clench in the muscles of your mouth and face. Feel a flow of energy going up from the perineum to the crown of your head. Breathe energy through the core of your body.

Feel yourself centering in length, the dimension of dignity. Let your spine fluidly expand or contract as it needs to, as you find your center.

Feel yourself centering in width, the dimension of connection, and permeability. How connected with others do you want to be? How withdrawn and solitary? Center in your skin.

Feel yourself centering in depth, the dimension of time. Give acknowledgement to all that is behind you. The ancestors, the personal history, the natural processes that brought you into this present moment. Feel into all that is within you—the intricate biophysical processes, the yearnings, the learnings, the power and potential. Feel into all that is before you. What does the future hold?

Feel yourself centering in purpose. Remember your intention for sexual wholeness. See it in your mind's eye.

From this place of center, feel yourself fierce and flowing. Affirm, 'I deserve joy. Joy matters.'

Exercise 16: Stand your ground

Simply feel your feet on the ground, almost like suction cups. Notice the springiness or stiffness in your legs. With feet firmly planted, like a well-rooted tree, sway slowly from the ankles—from side to side, from front to back. Keep your balance as you sway, feeling into the limits of possibility. How far from your personal center can you safely sway, in this particular stance, at this particular moment? Feel the pull in you to keep coming back to center.

Exercise 17: Sitting and grounding

Sit with your hands on your lower belly and your feet planted solidly on the ground. This is a posture in which both feet are on the floor and your spine is straight, but not rigidly so. Uncrossed legs allow the flow of energy to pass freely through the body. Your hands may be resting on your thighs or on the arms of the chair. Notice the position of your neck and head. Notice your sitz bones in the chair. Feel your genitals touching the chair. Notice your feet resting on the floor. Feel roots extending from the soles of your feet into the ground: through the floor, the soil layer, the rock layer and the crystal layer, deep into the center of the earth. Feel the heat. Bring up the energy from the center of the earth through all the layers of this beautiful planet, into your feet, your ankles, calves, thighs and pelvis. Feel the heat in your lower belly. Let it swirl in your pelvic bowl. Imagine it warming your genitals. Rock on your sitz bones. Bring one hand down to hold your genitals and the other up to hold your heart. Come to stillness and breathe into your hands.

Exercise 18: Animal exercise

Place your hands on an animal's body and feel the calmness of the animal. If you have a cat, dog or other companion animal that will allow you—rest your head on its chest, and listen for the heartbeat. Feel the breathing, and attune your energy to the energy of the animal. Feel your body settle into the animal's rhythm, calmness and groundedness

Variation: Do this exercise with a tree.

Exercise 19: Grounding in the present moment through breathing

Think of your breath as an anchor that holds you in the present moment. Breath awareness guides you back to the here and now when your mind wanders to the past or worries about the future. Breathe in and attend to the feeling of breathing in; breathe out and attend to the feeling of breathing out. By putting your attention on your breathing, you create space to live in the present moment. You may want to focus on the air coming in and out of your nostrils, on your skeleton expanding and contracting as you breathe. Try to slow down your breath, and practice waiting at the end of your exhale. You may also want to say calming, grounding statements to yourself as you breathe, like:

> Inhaling: 'Breathing in, I am calm.'
> Exhaling: 'Breathing out, I am safe.'

Notice this present-moment awareness as a refuge you can always come home to by anchoring your awareness with your breath.

Exercise 20: Comforting stillness

Stillness is another way to bring a sense of grounded safety to your physiology. Try hiding under the covers and slowing down your breath. Try wrapping your arms around your body and hugging yourself, just being still. Try being still in a fetal position. Try holding/spooning a safe person, or a beloved pet.

Exercise 21: Comforting movement

Deliberate movement is another way to bring a sense of grounded safety to your physiology. Try discerning any small movement impulses in your body and making them bigger. Let an impulse to wiggle a toe become a wildly kicking foot. Make fidgeting bigger, until it becomes dancing. Movement impulses can signal sympathetic nervous system hyperarousal. Reassure your nervous system by letting your body know that you are free and you can move. Try maintaining awareness of your body's centerline as you move.

Exercise 22: Other grounding techniques

Stamp your feet. Feel the power in your legs. Look up, look out, look around.

Hold, look at, listen to and/or smell an object that comforts you and reminds you of who you are. Create a 'Grounding and Centering' kit you can always turn to for comfort. Some examples of objects that may belong in your kit:

- a stone that you've found
- a photograph of a beloved person or animal who is unfailingly supportive
- a favorite talisman or piece of jewelry that serves as a symbol of sexual wholeness
- a photo of a special place that represents safety and comfort
- a poem that inspires

SELF-SOOTHING AND SELF-STIMULATION

Most people develop a repertoire of self-soothing and self-stimulating behaviors unconsciously. We need these self-regulating behaviors to calm and comfort or to arouse our physiology in times of autonomic nervous system hyperarousal or hypoarousal. Sometimes the behaviors we fall into do not serve us well in the long run. Eating sugary foods, starving, binging, cutting, smoking, drinking, yelling and having sex can all serve as self-regulating activities that temporarily calm and comfort an agitated nervous system, or stimulate a sense of aliveness when we feel dead and numb. Such behaviors can feel compulsive, because we literally cannot abide with the physiological distress we feel in the wake of trauma and neglect.

By learning to listen to our physiology and purposefully engage in self-regulating behaviors, we gain more choice. We will be increasingly able to engage in behaviors we truly enjoy, as we improve the baseline level of comfort we feel inside our skins.

Exercise 24: Let's get physical

Self-regulating behaviors need to be physical in order to regulate the autonomic nervous system.

We may find we are already engaging in self-regulating behaviors naturally and unconsciously. Finger and foot-tapping, rocking, blinking and playing with objects are ways to self-regulate autonomic nervous system arousal. By tuning into what happens in our bodies as we engage in these behaviors, we gain more awareness of the calming and/or enlivening effect they have on our physiology.

Walk. Run. Skip rope. Play ball. Put on some music and dance. Notice changes in your muscle tension, posture, heartbeat and breath. What is calming and comforting to your body? How are you stimulated to feel more vital and alive?

Exercise 25: Engage the senses

What soothing and enlivening activities engage your senses—sight, smell, hearing, taste and touch? Enjoy looking at a beautiful scene, smelling a home-cooked meal, listening to your favorite music, savoring the taste of something delicious, having a bubble bath, or receiving a pedicure. While an activity might primarily engage one sense, check in with the other senses too. What are you experiencing in your body? Notice if you feel like you don't deserve these pleasures, or that you 'should' be doing something more important.

Exercise 26: Different strokes for different folks

Some people find running is a good way to calm down. For others running is a way of feeling more vitality and aliveness. And then there are people for whom high-energy exercise triggers a sense of autonomic nervous system distress. For some, savoring an ice cream is a path of pure embodied bliss. For others, it is a way to trigger shame, or a cascade of sugar-induced unwanted symptoms. Feel into your own body in different situations for the self-regulating behaviors that are right for you. Find the right balance between habit and learning. Build a repertoire of 'go-to' self-regulating behaviors you know will work, and keep expanding what is possible by trying something new.

Exercise 27: Involve others

Performing acts of kindness and generosity enliven and comfort the nervous system of the giver. Touching and holding an animal or person, or being touched and held, help us feel grounded, valued and right with the world. Notice if you expect or 'need' to have your soothing come from others. If reaching out to others is your 'go-to' response to autonomic nervous system distress, can you add some more independent behaviors to your self-soothing repertoire? If reaching out to others is hard for you, enjoy the challenge in manageable doses.

Exercise 28: Involve sex and orgasm

If sex with other humans seems distressing, masturbation can be a great way of self-soothing for some people. Self-touch that integrates the genitals can help comfort and enliven body and being, even when desire for sex is low or nil (as it often is in people with high cortisol levels and chronic nervous system distress).

Some days you might comfort yourself with tender touch; other days you might want something more vigorous and 'nasty.' Sometimes it's nice to play with low levels of arousal over an extended period; other days you might go for a quick orgasm. Some people find porn-supported masturbation is blissful, while others find it disturbing. Powerful vibrators can be used to relax and enliven the body, including the genitals. As you mindfully masturbate, explore the differences between what is soothing and what is enlivening. Where is the comfort, and where is the learning in your self-pleasuring practice?

Exercise 29: Involve singing and dancing

Singing is a natural way to elevate our feelgood neurochemistry. Endorphins and oxytocin get activated, and cortisol levels are reduced, relieving anxiety and supporting a sense of wellbeing. Study after study has shown that singing soothes distress, lessens feelings of loneliness and depression, and contributes to quality of life. And you don't have to be a 'good' singer to enjoy all these benefits to body and soul!

If you really feel you can't sing, you can still enjoy benefits by imagining yourself singing while listening to some favorite music. For a more challenging version of this practice, try joining a choir.

Dancing in rhythm with music and with others is another proven way to both calm and stimulate the autonomic nervous system.

Exercise 30: Invoke spirit

Focusing on your sense of meaning can be soothing and enlivening. You might find your physiology and emotions can be soothed by refocusing on what is truly important to you. You might find peace through a sense of the sacred, or a spiritual connection to a higher power.

In many ancient and indigenous cultures, sexual energy is considered to be creative life force energy. Can you imagine weaving sexual energy into your sense of the divine?

CULTIVATE THE COMPASSIONATE WITNESS

Just as trauma and neglect have a huge impact on our autonomic nervous system, so do compassion and kindness. Viewing one's own emotions, thoughts and actions with loving detachment will foster wellbeing, flexibility, peace and aliveness in brain, body, and relationships. But anxious rumination, negative self-judgment, and intrusive, distracting, distressing thoughts are typical for survivors of trauma and neglect.

Cultivating 'compassionate witness' consciousness means creating an environment of loving kindness *within* us. We can gain an ability to step away from identification with our thoughts and feelings. We learn to feel our feelings and think our thoughts without becoming attached to them. For example, we may feel ashamed of some sexual desire or experience. Without witness consciousness, this might lead to anxious rumination about how this desire has damaged our own or others' lives, and how we might fix that. With witness consciousness, we might simply and kindly notice our feeling of shame.

We might be caught in obsessive thoughts about someone who hurt us. Without witness consciousness, we might plan just how to confront and change this person, or castigate ourselves for being vulnerable. With witness consciousness, we might simply and kindly notice the feeling of being hurt.

When someone is angry with us, and we don't have a strong compassionate witness within us, we might go into autonomic nervous system hyperarousal, and try to stay safe by defending ourselves, getting away, trying to appease them, or dissociating. With witness consciousness, we can feel safer staying fully present with strong emotions in others as well as in ourselves. We can kindly and compassionately invite feelings to be expressed, without needing to react to them or fix them. Our own emotional distress, and others', feels less threatening. We can have more curiosity and receptivity to new experiences, instead of being ruled by fear.

Yes, sometimes it is important to fight for change, defend ourselves, or take steps to repair harm we have done to others or ourselves. However, we can do this from a place of choice. Cultivating compassionate witness consciousness gives us that choice. Instead of reacting on the basis of our thoughts and feelings, or others' thoughts and feelings, we can simply notice. We can offer time and caring attention to what is unfolding within and around us. Instead of being focused on trying to change things, we can set a goal of equanimity with all we cannot change. In this way, we can be compassionate with our failures to come from a place of compassionate witness. No one does this perfectly!

Standard meditation instructions guide us to cultivate witness consciousness with a focus on breath (body sensation, candle, sound, or something other than our chattering minds). As thoughts and feelings pass through our minds we can simply notice, bringing our attention gently back to the breath. But people dealing with a history of trauma and neglect may need a different approach. Being unable to focus attention and filter out irrelevant information is one of the common consequences of chronic trauma. The following exercises can help to cultivate the compassionate witness with active meditations and alternative approaches.

Exercise 31: Witness collage

Set your intention to connect with the compassionate witness within yourself. Gather collage materials: glue, scissors, magazines with lots of pictures, and a base to glue them down on. Sit quietly with an open mind. With a sense of open inquiry into the character of the compassionate witness, look through the pictures you have assembled. Is there some image that resonates with your intention? Is there an image that picks you? If no image comes for you today, no need to force it. If an image finds you, or several images, make a collage that shows the compassionate witness. Then when you are feeling swept away by a challenging situation or by your own thoughts and feelings, you can recall or study this image, and invite it to occupy your mind.

Exercise 32: Finding your power animal

Every animal has a different energy and a different range of symbolic meanings. Through creative imagination and listening to the world around us, we can find 'power animals' that bring their particular energy into our lives. Power animals can help and guide us. They are allies to protect us as we navigate new territories of body and soul on our journey to sexual wholeness.

What animal 'comes' to you when you sit quietly, with an open mind?

What animal literally comes to you, perhaps as a bug in your bed or a pest in the attic? What animal, bird or insect has fascinated you in the past? Which are you especially interested in now?

Consider animals big and small. Think of majestic eagles and enormous elephants, and also of dragonflies and mosquitoes. It's not only the glamorous animals that can be our allies. Frogs, slugs and tiny protozoa are powerful animals too.

Do you look at things from a hawk's perspective, or a wren's? Do you dance like a butterfly or sting like a bee? Are you playful? Fancy? Plain? Awkward? Do you yearn to travel, or do you like to stay in familiar territory? Do you relate most to air, earth or water? Are there animals in your awareness that have similar qualities?

Once you have chosen an animal, read about its behaviors and symbolic meanings. Consider how its medicine relates to the vision you have for your sexual wholeness.

Honor your power animal by drawing a picture of it or collaging pictures from magazines and the Internet. Allow new insights to emerge through this process. Write about why you chose this animal to be your power animal, the affinity you feel, the insights it offers, and how it will support you on your journey.

Exercise 33: Plant teacher

Just as animals can be allies, so can plants.

Find a plant in your own environment that calls to you. Interact with the plant. Smell, feel, and if you are sure this is a non-toxic plant, taste it. Consider how it looks—is it big and powerful, or small and delicate? Is it deeply rooted, or lightly bound with earth? Think of its life cycle, how it grows from seed or rhizome, how it interacts with light, air and water. How does awareness of this plant resonate with your own cells? We share much of our DNA with plants.

Read about the plant's properties and how it was used for food or healing by indigenous cultures.

How does this plant's particular properties—its grace, shape, color, reproductive strategy, and medicinal properties—relate to the vision you have for your sexual wholeness?

Create a way to honor the plant and keep it in your awareness. You might make a drawing, or put a branch in a vase. The plant can be an ally who is always accessible, comforting and guiding you on your journey.

Exercises 34–35: Guided meditations

It can be helpful to listen to guided meditations or meditate following a specific inquiry rather than trying to meditate without structure.

Egg meditation

Begin by looking at an egg. Focus on the egg, and let its exquisite shape envelop your awareness. Close your eyes, and feel the egg in its wholeness, an ancient symbol of the world, of creation, spring, and fertility in many cultures and religions. An egg incubates new life. It is a safe, nurturing environment that holds and protects its contents through the process of becoming.

Think of the forms, environments and relationships that hold you safe in your process of becoming. Feel the safety of your safe places. Feel the protection and nurturance of the wondrous containers you are growing into, growing within.

How can you go on becoming more and more fully what you are, within these exquisite containers that give you a name, a home, a place for becoming? How can you accept the nurturance? How can you inhabit your eggshells fully?

An egg incubates new life, and then, it becomes a prison that has to be broken open, so that new life can emerge. Is a particular eggshell getting small, and cramped? Does it feel like something you need to shatter? Not knowing what is outside and beyond this environment that has allowed and supported you, dare to crack the eggshell, as you are driven into a wild openness by your own process of becoming what you are.

Let the images and information come to you without judgment. Allow the gift.

Volcano meditation

Sit and visualize being a breathing volcano, alive and vital, yet massive and unmoving, completely what you are, a centered, grounded presence aware of the genital energy inside you. Feel the genital generator quiet and smoldering. Feel a flash of energy, movement or tingling, liquefaction warm within. Experience the sweetness of the invisible inner fire, moment-by-moment, constantly changing, yet always being just itself. The volcano's magnificence and beauty are not changed one bit by the weather, or the passage of days. It is there whether people see it or not. The fire within will erupt only when it's ready, and not before. Breathe into the fire within.

Exercise 36: Touch as witness

Kindly and compassionately touch yourself. Or receive kind, compassionate touch from a professional massage therapist or a friend. Stay quiet and focus on your experience during the massage instead of chatting. Absorb a sense of being witnessed and cared for into your cells.

Exercise 37: A safe container for sorrow and challenge

with thanks to Michele Wong

Find a special little box or bag for this ritual. Write down troubling feelings, distracting thoughts, obsessions, anxieties and fears on separate pieces of paper. Consider each paper with kindness, and place it into the container. Close the container up. Notice you are honoring painful emotions without needing to fix them. You can put feelings and thoughts into the container whenever you need to. Remember that the container can always be opened when it is safe to do so, and emptied when the time is right.

Exercise 38: Your own safe place

Do you have or can you imagine a place in the world where you feel safe? Picture it in great detail. Recall or envision the feeling of your feet on the ground there, the textures and smells of plants or fabrics, the temperature, the light. Breathe in the feeling of this safe place, into every cell. Find a picture or make a collage that reminds you of this safe place. Remember you can come back here any time you want.

Exercise 39: How are you resourced?

adapted from Peter Levine

Look again at the map you drew called 'My sexual wholeness' in Exercise 1. Consider whether to add more details, ideas, feelings and images to your map. Now feel into resources that are available to you on this journey.

You have inner resources. Think of all that is within you. You are resourced by your own willingness, kindness, health, courage and creativity. You have personal history and desire to guide you. Perhaps you have learning you embody, practices you have established, credentials you have earned, or skills you have identified. Notice that your woundedness is also a gift. It guides you to this deep emotional and spiritual journey with your sexuality.

You have external resources. Think of all that is around you. Are there relationships or places that sustain you? Perhaps you have food on the table, money in the bank, or underwear that helps you feel sexy. Perhaps there is a sex toy that works, a private place to meditate or masturbate. Perhaps this book is a resource for you.

'Emerging resources' refers to things you have identified as *potentially* important resources. Are there practices you want to make into habits? Are there relationship possibilities that might be joyful? Is there an underwear store near you, or online, where you might find something that helps you feel sexy? Is there a workshop you could sign up for, or a teaching you want to explore?

Describe how you are resourced. Pay attention to how thinking about each resource feels in your body.

Internal resources (what is inside you)	**External resources** (what is around you)	**Possible and emerging resources** (what you are finding and beginning)

Exercise 40: Fortress of love mandala

with thanks to Kristin Lang

Graphics with a design within a circle are often referred to as mandalas, the Sanskrit word for 'circle.' The circle is an ancient sacred form that helps us access our inner knowledge that we are connected with all life. Drawing mandalas is a form of meditation and can be very soothing. Mandalas have long been used in psychotherapy to communicate emotions and explore and integrate new ideas.

The inquiry with this mandala drawing is 'How can you build an imaginal fortress of love to surround and protect you?' Consider what you love. Consider your personal energy and power, your light and darkness. What are your personal symbols? Your heartfelt values? What protects you? Use colors, images and words to fill the INSIDE of the mandala with love.

Consider what threatens you and name it or draw it OUTSIDE your fortress. Consider how your anger at those threatening forces can fuel your true power. Craft a declaration of your will and intentions about who you are and what or who is allowed to be in YOUR space.

You can fill in a plain circle, or use the mandala pattern on the next page, to create a 'fortress of love' mandala.

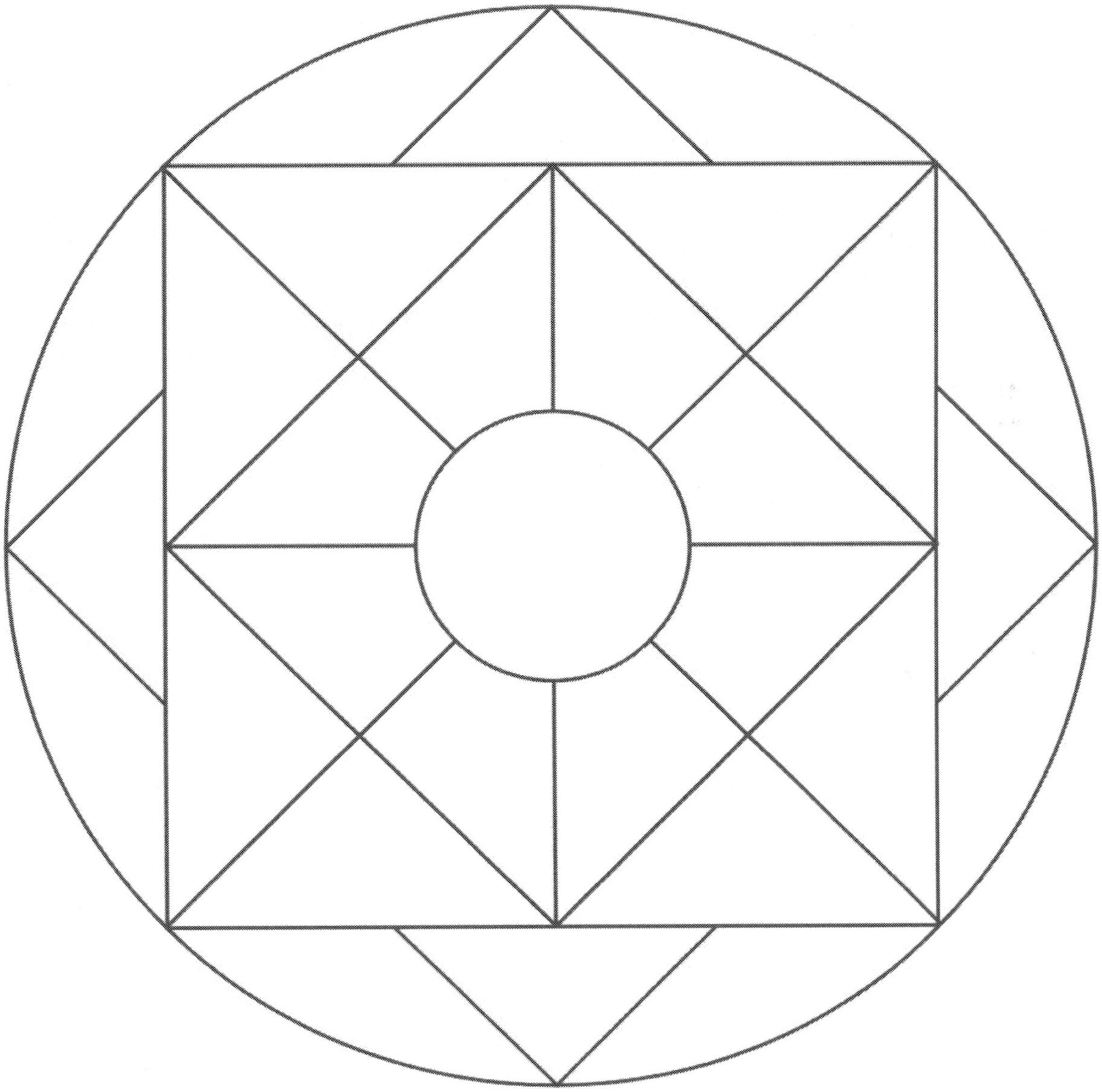

Integrating Brain and Body

We are taught to separate mind from body, to value cognitive function and ignore visceral function. People grow up thinking they can and should repress gut feelings and body yearnings, and express their sexuality in ways that answer to voices around them and in their heads. Dissociation, minimization of body sensation and numbing are ways we adapt to living with cultural norms.

Neuroscience affirms the somatic understanding that the living, sensing, self-sensing being is embodied. We experience, evaluate and remember the world with our whole bodies, exploring and responding with fingers, breath, heart, guts, asshole and skin. Physical processes *are* emotional, cognitive and spiritual processes. We encounter and assess the world with neurotransmitters and neurohormones that course through our bodies, creating moods, energies and ecstasies as they regulate and dysregulate body functions.

Each person is also embedded in a world of relationships with other humans, with culture, personal and social history, and the environment. We think and feel through the energy and information of relationships. Oppressions and privileges have a deep impact our feelings and thoughts, and our everyday behaviors reflect, reinforce, or open possibilities for change in the power structures of our families and communities. Our needs, yearnings and physiological functions keep us in a continual, dynamic exchange between self and not-self. We exist in the flow of nature and spirit.

Living with somatic awareness means consciously tuning into this "embodied and embedded" self (in Daniel Siegel's words), paying attention to body sensations and consciously integrating brain and body. We can begin actively noticing sensation, temperature, pressure, movement impulse, numbness, breath and pelvic clench. We can notice what moods and emotions we hold in posture, gut, voice, facial expression, genitals, sweat, heartbeat and saliva. We can also notice how these embodied emotions show up in ways we live or fail to live our passions and commitments, and in how we construct our stories and our prayers. With more conscious awareness of body sensations, we can live in greater understanding of our unconscious reactions, habitual patterns, inner yearnings and environmental assessments. We can consider how and when we embody oppressions and where we embody resilience and transformations. Our body, if we pay attention, *is* our soul. It is a way of knowing and exploring intricate dimensions in an unfolding relationship between self and world, world and self.

Living 'in our heads' is an attentional focus that empowers us to function despite nervous system distress. It is both a personal survival strategy and a cultural pattern. But, living a disembodied life means that we will miss opportunities to connect deeply, feel passionately, and explore the erotic in ways that integrate all of who we are.

BODY-BRAIN INTEGRATION

The capacity to be aware of body sensation needs to be built gradually, with attention to each person's personal learning zone.

Exercise 41: Basic body scan

Close your eyes and bring your attention to your body. Breathe.

Interior scan: First bring your awareness to the cascade of sensation within the body. Notice temperature, pressure, vibration, movement or movement impulse, heartbeat, belly, sore places, and feelings of pleasure. Scan for sensations through the body from toes to head.

Scan the Skin: Notice the air touching your skin. Notice the contact between your body and the world around you: feet on the floor, bum on the chair, arms resting on belly.

Scan the Interconnections: Notice your breathing. Notice the rise and fall of your chest and belly. Notice how you are held by gravity. Check in with your senses. What do you hear, see (inside your eyelids), smell, taste, touch?

Scan your Mental Activity. Notice any thoughts flitting through your mind with non-attachment.

Centering: Bring your awareness to the center of your body, your pelvis. Hold your awareness in your pelvic bowl. Anchor your attention with your breath.

Exercise 42: Mindful walking with genital focus

Begin by standing still and becoming aware of your body. Notice your stance and your posture, feel the weight of your body on the ground, become aware of all the subtle movements involved in standing upright. Notice your skeleton expanding and contracting with your breath. Notice the feeling of clothes on your body. Allow your knees to bend very slightly and feel your hips as your center of gravity. Focus your awareness on your pelvic bowl and your genitals. See if you can feel your genitals from the inside with your breath, and from the outside as your clothes rest and brush against your genitals.

Allow your eyes to focus softly ahead of you, taking in the world around you so you feel safe-enough moving through it. Now slowly begin to walk. Notice how you start by lifting one foot and balancing on the other. Try to maintain a soft body and breathing awareness as you walk. Keep tuning in to the sensations in your genitals. Let the movement of your legs stimulate your genital nerves. Feel the clothes moving over your thighs, buttocks, and genitals. Feel the proximity of your hands and your genitals and if it feels right to do so, allow your hands to brush up against your genitals or rest in gentle genital contact as you walk.

When your attention drifts away from the walking and genital sensation, take notice of your thoughts and emotions without judgment. Gently guide your awareness back.

Continue your mindful walking with a genital focus for anywhere from 5 to 20 minutes.

When it's time to end the meditation, pause, once again experiencing yourself standing still.

Exercise 43: Get triggered

Use an environmental cue to trigger a regular check-in with the cascade of sensation inside your body. Let ending a phone call or buckling your seatbelt function as a trigger for a body scan. Scan from toes to head, and then let your attention settle for a moment in your pelvis. Shake your hips if you are standing, or wiggle your pelvis in the chair. Notice any genital sensation. Savour.

Exercise 44: Inner smile

Breathe and relax, then allow a soft smile to emerge and shape your lips. Feel the smile radiate up into your eyes, ears, brain, the back of your head. Let it wrinkle your nose. Bring the smile down your throat, into your lungs and breasts, into your belly, into your pelvis. Feel your genitals smile. Send the smile down into your legs and feet, your arms and hands.

Send the smile deeper. Feel all your trillions of cells smile. Imagine them all like microscopic happy faces, smiling inside you. Smile at the trillions of microbes who live on you and within you, and without which you could not live. Imagine them all smiling back.

Feel any movement impulse in the smiling, and express this by wiggling, shaking, clenching and unclenching, dancing, or doing nothing at all.

Exercise 45: Shall we dance?

People who carry trauma and neglect in their physiology may have difficulties with movement, coordination and sensing where their bodies are in space. The kinesthetic sense is impaired. The social dance that we are all always engaged in can feel like an impossible challenge when we were not lovingly taught how to move in rhythm with others. Experiences and practices that allow the nervous system to gradually build capacity to process proprioceptive information can be soothing and enlivening.

Try this:

Jump on a trampoline.

Lie beneath heavy blankets, feeling how your body relates to the environment.

Try pushing: press your hands against each other, push down into a chair with your pelvic floor, push down with your feet when you are standing, push up into the sky with your head and arms, push against a wall.

Try pushing with a safe person who can push against you. Experience what it's like to push back instead of collapse and surrender.

Try pulling. Pull your hands apart. Pull a heavy weight up a hill. Pull something or someone you really want toward you. Feel what it's like to really pull something toward you instead of waiting for whatever comes your way.

Stretch your body with a yoga pose. Feel into stretch. Now relax. Feel the sense of every muscle, tendon and blood vessel letting go. Feel the sense of ease.

Ride a bicycle. Notice how you feel differently riding when it's easy and when you need to be forceful.

Dance where and when you cannot make a mistake, dance when no one is watching. You might try Contact Improv, Five Rhythms, Dance Temple, or partner dances.

UP AND DOWN BRAIN INTEGRATION

I use the common metaphor of the 'triune brain' when explaining the structure of the brain to clients and students. Although it is an oversimplified representation, the 'triune brain' is a useful fiction for describing how three billion years of evolutionary wisdom live in our brains and bodies.

At the top of the spinal cord, the brainstem can be described as the ancient 'reptilian brain.' This part of the brain coordinates heartbeat, breathing, digestion, balance, and other basic life-sustaining functions. It is involved in reflexive and instinctive behaviors: feeding, fighting, fleeing, and fucking—'the four F's'—to which I add a fifth: 'find your way home.'

The limbic system, right above the 'reptilian brain,' can be described as the 'mammalian brain.' It is more developed in mammals that care for vulnerable young. This is the seat of attachment, emotion and visceral regulation. It is involved in the emotional bonding between lovers, and caring for loved ones through prolonged relationships. Vocal communication and play behaviors are governed here. It also monitors and remembers danger.

Together the 'mammalian brain' and the 'reptilian brain' make up the 'emotional brain.' Intricate emotions—love and fear, rage and anguish—are embodied in us through neurochemicals generated by the functions of these subcortical brain structures.

The cortical structures of the rational, cognitive brain—what we think of as the 'human brain' (although similar to other primates and dwarfed by the cortical structures of whales)—are a relatively recent development in evolutionary history. The cerebral cortex is where stories about what we want and feel get developed, and conscious decisions about what to do get made. It is where people develop insight about their sexual experiences, and imagine and plan their erotic future. It is where we consciously perceive sensory information and decide what we want our bodies to do.

Through trauma and neglect, these various aspects of brain function can get disconnected from each other; their capacity to work together can be impaired.

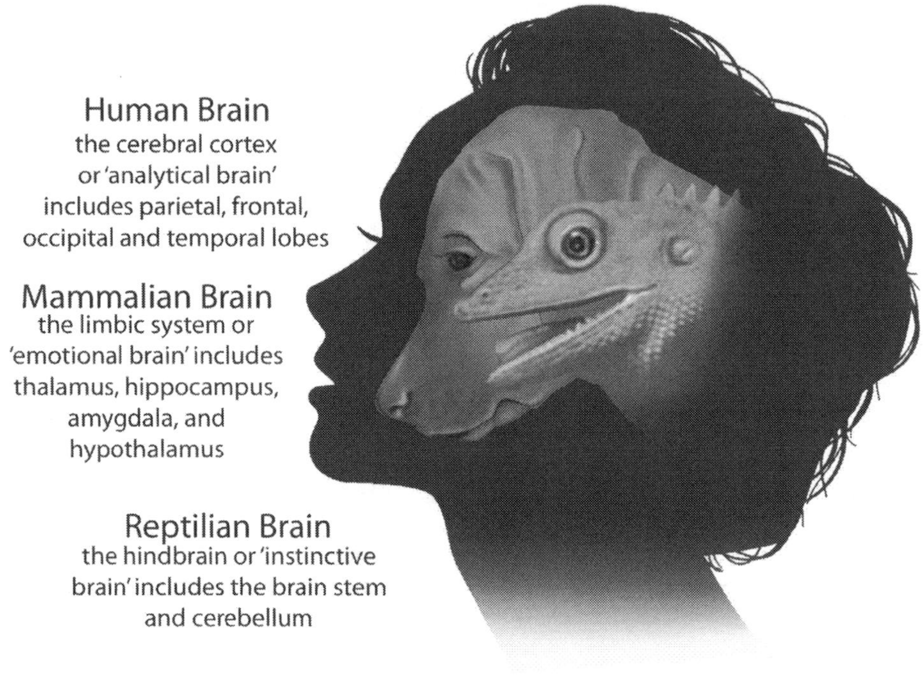

Figure 7: The Triune Brain

Survivors of sexual trauma and neglect can find overwhelming emotional responses overriding their conscious choices around sex. 'Amygdala hijack' is term coined (by Daniel Goleman) to explain the process through which this happens in the brain. Figure 8 shows an optical stimulus going to the thalamus. From there, information is relayed to the amygdala (part of the limbic system or 'mammalian brain') and also to the cerebral cortex, or 'human brain.' As information travels the tiny extra distance to the cerebral cortex, it is already being evaluated by the amygdala. If the record of experiences stored in the hippocampus tells the amygdala that what's ahead is dangerous, the amygdala triggers the HPA (hypothalmic-pituitary-adrenal) axis and the body is flooded with stress hormones. The 'mammalian brain' processes information milliseconds earlier than the 'human brain.'

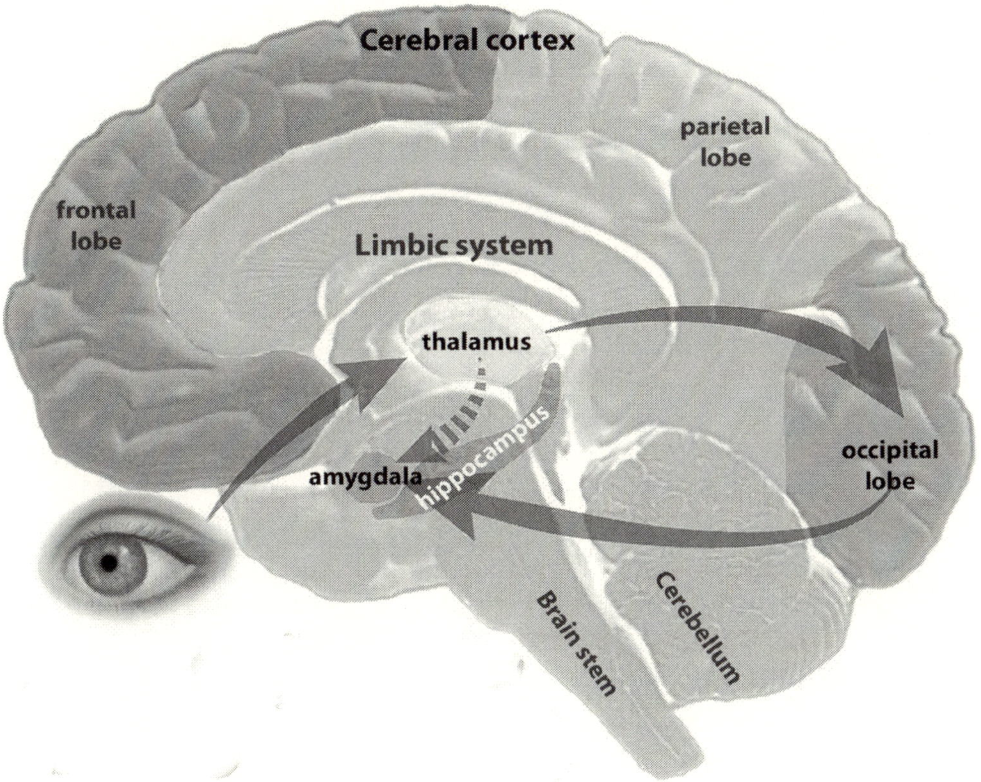

Figure 8: Amygdala hijack
based on a drawing by ManosHacker, 2011, creative commons licensing, modified by Caffyn Jesse.

EXERCISES FOR UP AND DOWN BRAIN INTEGRATION: ALIGNING INSTINCTS, EMOTIONS AND THOUGHTS

Exercise 46: Finding Yes and No in our bodies

with thanks to Dr. Liam 'Captain' Snowdon

In this exercise we begin to learn what 'Yes!' and 'No!' feel like in our bodies. We practice giving voice to what we feel, and feeling the autonomic nervous system activation that comes from resisting what we don't want, or claiming what we want.

Go slowly and softly enough to enjoy the experience, which can bring up unexpected yearnings and painful memories.

Ground and center yourself.

Find a sense of No and how that feels in your body. How does your body express a No? What are the many ways of saying No—fierce, angry, soft, tentative, apologetic, straightforward, casual, emphatic, empathic..... ? If you can't find a No inside yourself, see if you can find it on behalf of someone else, someone to whom an injustice is being done. Is there a No in you to protect a beloved child? Express your No physically and with your tones of voice.

Come to stillness, shake off those feelings, ground and center yourself.

Find a sense of Yes and how that feels in your body. How does your body express its Yes? What are the many ways of saying Yes? Try on a Yes that is huge and expansive. Feel for one that is sweet and small. There could be an emphatic Yes, a tentative yes and a YES that is angry and forceful. Express your Yes physically. Move and use your arms and legs. Express your Yes with different tones of voice.

Come to stillness, shake off those feelings, ground and center yourself.

Reflect on whether it is hard to access No or Yes. Are there habitual ways of saying No and Yes that are embedded in your nervous system?

Exercise 47: Play fight

Work with a partner and 'play fight' with your words. We can playfully feel into autonomic nervous system activation by deliberately engaging the fight response.

Decide who is 'A' and who is 'B.' Put a timer on for one minute, and then switch roles.

A: Yes!

B: No!

A: Yes I can!
B: No you can't!

A: No you won't!
B: Yes I will!

A: No I won't!
B: Yes you will!

What does it feel like to encounter resistance? What barriers do you feel in your body, as you play with feeling and expressing your inner fire? How are you willing and unwilling to fight for what you believe in? Does the gender identity of the person you are partnered with for this exercise have an impact on what it feels like to do it? Think back to the goals and intentions you set for this journey to sexual wholeness. What would it feel like to fight for what you want?

Exercise 48: Play flight

adapted from Peter Levine

This exercise is designed to give you an imaginary experience of fleeing an unsafe situation, escaping with your life, and coming back to a sense of safety.

Take a deep breath, ground and center. Close your eyes and imagine that you are a prey animal. Pick an animal you feel an affinity with.

Sense danger in the air, and identify it. You might be a small bird chased by a hawk, an elephant being chased by human hunters, an antelope fleeing from a pride of lions.

Feel the strength in your legs or wings. Feel the panic surging through your body. Run! Flee to a place of safety. Stay hidden and quiet, barely breathing, until the danger passes.

Dare to look up at last, and recognize—you have escaped. The predators are gone. Feel the escape in your body. Feel the fear subside. Notice your heartbeat settling. Feel the tension in your muscles letting go. Take a deep breath. Look around you. If you are shaking and trembling, that's good. Let it happen.

Stretch and shake off the experience. Imagine you are the animal resuming your day.

Reflections: What does it feel like to run away, and save yourself? Are there barriers inside you to escaping situations and people who are harmful? Are you already a great escape artist? Do you usually escape by fleeing and hiding, or do you escape by going numb and dissociating within a frightening situation?

Variation: Do with a partner, or in a group.

Exercise 48: Play with your inner turtle

On a beach in Mexico I watched newly-hatched baby turtles scramble across the beach to the ocean. Air was new to them. Water was unknown to them. Yet somehow they knew they must get home to the sea. They scrambled over the sand, facing enormous dangers. Finally they reached the water, where breaking waves pushed them back, again and again. Still these tiny reptiles kept struggling to come home.

Some profound wisdom exists in these reptilian brains. An urge to find an environment where they can grow fully into their potential; a courage to face enormous dangers; a persistence despite gigantic setbacks; an inner knowing there is a home they have never experienced—all these are wisdoms I want for my life.

Create a 'turtle mandala' on the next page, using words, colors and images to reflect positively on your own instincts. What is your inner knowing? Where are you at home? What is the food you need to nourish the person you are meant to be? What will you fight to defend? Who and what will you flee to stay safe and survive? Who do you want to fuck? How do you find your way home?

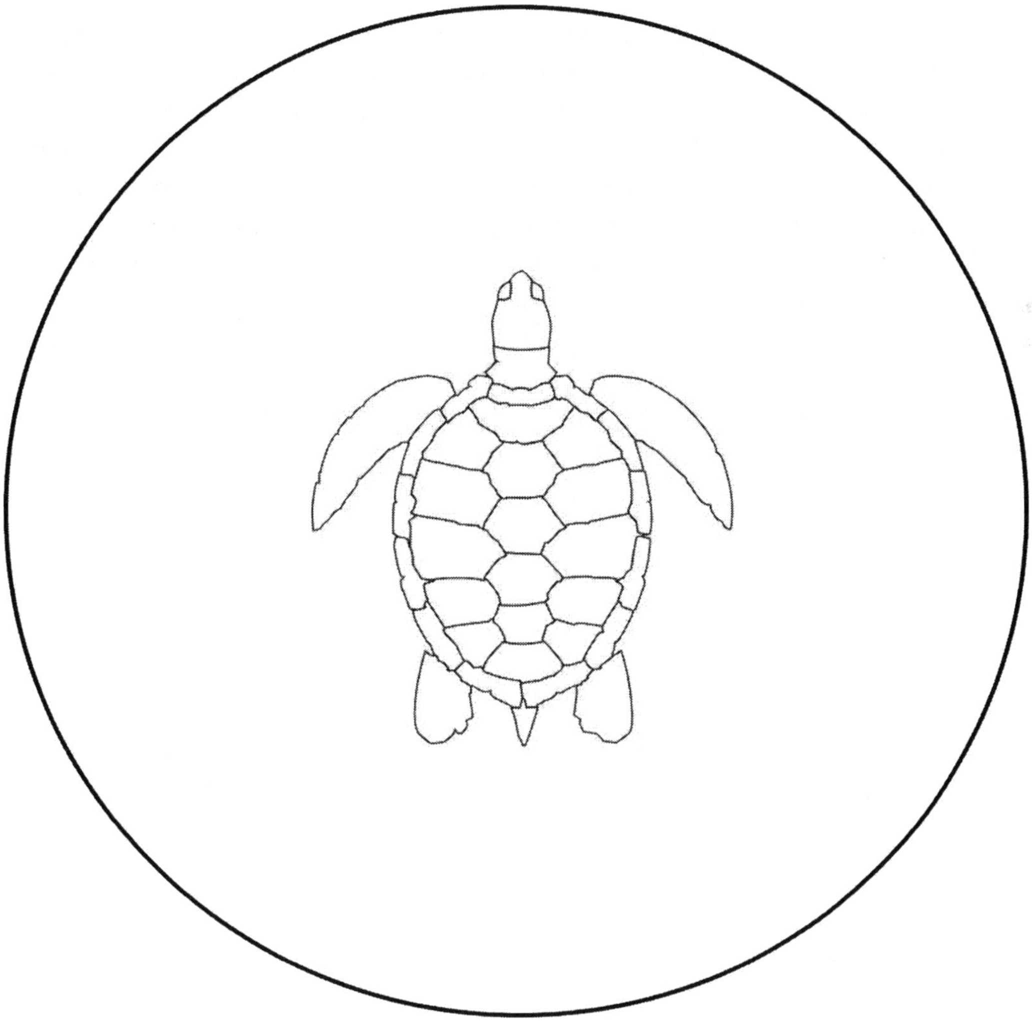

INTEGRATING LEFT AND RIGHT-BRAIN

As well as different functions in the 'reptilian, mammalian and human' aspects of the brain, the brain has some segregated functions between the left and right hemispheres. (Like the 'triune brain,' any generalized description of left and right-brain structures is a useful fiction that helps us understand and play with remarkably complex processes.)

Exercises aimed at integrating left and right brain functions can be an important aspect of a person's journey to sexual wholeness. The left brain has been described as the intuitive brain and supports action-oriented, risky behaviors. The right brain has been described as the rational brain and the home of caution and critical thinking.* A feeling of separation and alienation between these brain functions is a common legacy of trauma or neglect. Some survivors tend to make high-risk choices about sex while others feel restrained by excessive caution. Some feel afraid that opening the 'Pandora's Box' of sexuality will impair their rationality. We can use neural exercises to weave brain functions together and feel more whole.

*The popular notion that the left hemisphere is the logical brain and the right hemisphere is the creative brain is incorrect.

Therapists use a variety of techniques to help with integrating left and right brain functions. Approaches include Eye Movement Desensitization and Reprocessing (EMDR), Emotional Freedom Technique (EFT), art therapy, mind-mapping and using play, images, and movement.

Exercise 50: Integrating left and right-brain knowledge of the genitals

with thanks to Mehdi Dervish

Step 1: Drawing / looking without naming

Look at your genitals in a mirror, and draw them, without trying to make a 'good' drawing. Try to quiet mental chatter while you focus on the shapes you are seeing. Draw edges, and the spaces between different edges. Draw light and shadow. Notice the judgments that come up in your mind, about your genitals and about your drawing, and gently put them aside.

Step 2: Genital mapping

Compare your genitals with the genital anatomy drawings on the following page. Relate your own body parts to the labels on the anatomy drawing. Touch and hold each part while you name it.

Step 3: Let your genitals talk

Free-write a letter to your self from the point of view of your genitals. Clear your mind and relax your body as much as possible. Then just write for ten minutes. Write anything and everything that flows through you from your genitals. Write continuously and quickly. When the time limit is finished, stop. Have your genitals sign the letter, using whatever name they want to be known by in this moment.

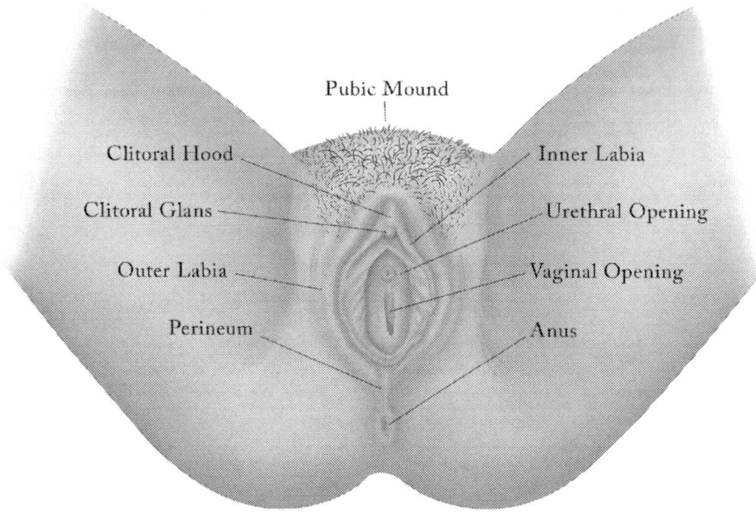

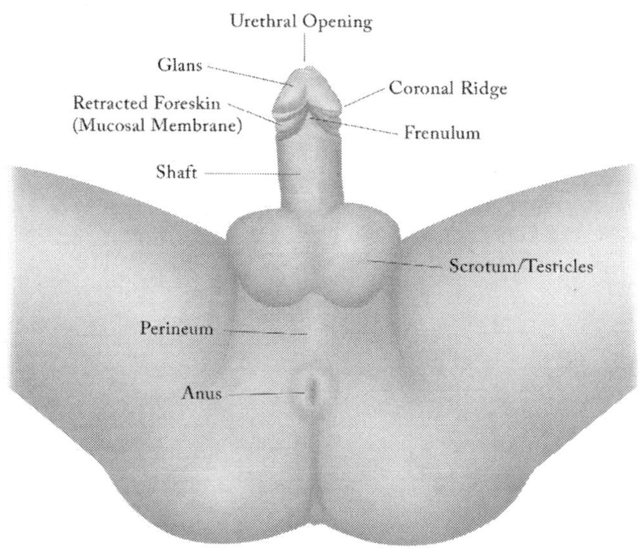

Figure 8: Anatomy of the external genitals

These drawings are schematic representations only. Genitals are as different as faces. A huge range of sizes, colors, shapes and configurations are normal and beautiful.

NARRATIVE INTEGRATION: THE WHOLE-BRAIN (AND HOLE-BRAIN) STORY

When we engage left and right brain in creating a narrative of our personal history, the storytelling process becomes very powerful.

Often we feel shame about our sexual histories. We feel shame about being victimized, or victimizing others, or both. We feel shame about having lots of sex or no sex or the wrong kind of sex. Our stories feel far too shameful to be told. So, we stay hidden, isolated and invisible. The yearning to know and be known is frozen and entombed. In shame and isolation, we lose connection with our emotional life.

Deepening access to feeling

A common way that people deal with personal histories of trauma and neglect is to say, 'It happened, but it doesn't matter.' One client, Karla, described being molested throughout her childhood by her father and grandfather, and then held captive and raped repeatedly as a young woman. With an unexpressive face and voice, she said, "It happened, but I don't think of it as trauma. It's just life. No big deal." Karla had the flat affect that is often a consequence of stuck trauma. In her, it was combined with a pattern of being highly reactive to mundane things that were seemingly of little consequence. Another client, Jack, was raped as a young man, and in subsequent decades struggled with addiction and made several suicide attempts. Jack told his story as if it didn't matter. He claimed to have dealt with it all, years before. While his words said he was over it, his demeanor was always agitated. His stories about other people would suddenly include violent images or metaphors. Jack did not feel like a trustworthy person.

I understand the lure of apathetic narrative. Who wants to be pathetic? Who wants to be defined by trauma? I myself was almost fifty before I could grieve a childhood that included sexual molestation and violence. Telling my story in different ways, letting myself be seen and touched, I shed skin after skin of shame and minimization, until finally I was bare enough to feel.

Can you use movement, music, drawing or collage to access more profound feelings about your sexual history? Deepen access to feeling as best you can, and know this is an iterative process. You can tell your story over and over, being courageous enough to eschew getting stuck in a static narrative that does not touch you. Let your story intensify emotionally as you build capacity to know your embodied feelings fully.

Memory and healing: integrating the holes

Some people have sharp and specific memories of sexual traumas they have endured. Others have only disconnected fragments of remembered trauma. Others simply wonder whether there could be sexual trauma in their personal history, because of the ways symptoms show up in their relationship with sex. Often people who do not remember clearly think the goal of therapy is to recover lost memories, and that if they remember details of the trauma it will be released.

You don't need to remember specifics of what happened. The majority of trauma survivors do not have sharp memories. Implicit memories can be held in the body and nervous system function without explicit conscious memory. Trauma actually causes damage in parts of the brain responsible for conscious memory. Exact memories of specific sexual traumas may be forever inaccessible.

Sometimes we need to tell our story in ways that include the holes in our story, letting go of any shame about not remembering.

Exercise 51: Using words, images and movement to tell your story

Write notes, and collage images or create a mind map about your experience of sex. Or create a dance to describe your story. Include the pain and suffering you endured, and any pain and suffering you inflicted on others. Be courageous, but stay within your learning zone.

Bring your notes and/or drawings and/or dance and tell your story to a safe person. Consider telling someone outside your friendship circle: a professional sex educator, registered clinical counselor, a psychotherapist, or someone who you know is trained to hear what you have to say with compassion and equanimity. If you cannot find a safe person, can you find a safe animal, tree, ancestor or imaginary friend? Let yourself be seen, and then feel yourself held in love, as all of who you are.

INTEGRATING GUT AND BRAIN

When we sense danger, digestive function shuts down as our autonomic nervous system prepares us to fight, flee, appease, freeze or dissociate. Stuck trauma can mean stuck digestive function, or over-function. We cannot properly digest our food when we sense danger everywhere.

People who have suffered sexual trauma have high levels of gastrointestinal (GI) disorders. Gastroesophageal Reflux Disease (GERD), irritable bowel syndrome, colitis and subdural reflux are among the GI disorders linked with trauma, depression and anxiety. Sexual trauma or neglect may underpin a struggle with addiction, eating disorders, disordered eating, and other conditions and behaviors that reflect a disconnection between body, soul and GI tract.

The vagus nerve is part of the way gut and brain communicate. If a good 'gut feeling' about the environment is communicated to the brain through the vagus nerve, the body can digest and absorb nutrients. When the vagus nerve is overstimulated by stress, activating a 'dissociate' response, blood pressure and heart rate drop and digestion stops.

The capacity of the vagus nerve to properly regulate organ function is indicated by 'heart rate variability.' You should experience a slight increase of heart rate when you inhale, and a slight decrease of heart rate when you exhale. The difference between heart rate on inhale and exhale is a measure of vagal tone. With trauma or neglect, and chronic agitation of the nervous system, heart rate and breath become disconnected and there is little or no heart-rate variability. Deep slow breathing with a very long exhale is a way to stimulate the vagus nerve and reweave connection between heart, breath, and gut feeling. Vagal tone is linked to physical and psychological wellbeing. A lack of vagal tone is linked to physical symptoms including inflammation and heart attacks, and psychological symptoms including negative moods and loneliness.

The 'gut-brain axis' is another communication route. The neuroscience term refers to the biochemical interaction between microbiota in the gut and the nervous system. Gut bacteria have co-evolved with humans and are essential to our survival. Trillions of these microbes help regulate digestion and metabolism and play a large role in the body's immune system. They interact with intestinal cells to produce about 90 per cent of the body's supply of serotonin, an important neurotransmitter that influences our perception of pleasure, as well as GI function. Though the relationship between neurotransmitters in the gut and the brain is a research frontier, it is known that gut bacteria affect mood and behavior. A healthy microbiome aids people in being calm and content. People can help reduce anxiety and depression by taking probiotics and eating food that supports a diverse and well-functioning microbiome. In turn, our moods and thoughts directly affect gut bacteria. Chronic stress can shift the environment of the gut in ways that lead to microbial imbalance, make us more vulnerable to infection, and create a feedback loop through the nervous system that generates increased anxiety and depression.

There is also a muscular component to GI dysfunction. The 'startle response' activates the pelvic clench we investigated earlier (see 'Doggie wisdom' and 'Portals to the autonomic nervous system'). Indeed, muscles all along the axis of the body from the jaw to the pelvis can become chronically clenched, inhibiting digestion, breathing and sexual function.

These and other aspects of the connection between gut and brain dance together with mystery and our inner knowing. Simply feeling into the complex ways our emotions and experiences get embodied through gut reactions is a useful and healing practice. Slowing down, savoring, listening to our bodies, eating good food, mindful pooping, and enjoying vigorous exercise are all ways to create increased integration of gut and brain. (Anal massage is another way to connect directly with the smooth muscle function of the digestive tract and open a portal to the autonomic nervous system. More on this in my book *Erotic Massage for Healing and Pleasure*.)

Changing our baseline physiology is not a quick fix. It's good to let go of any need to 'do it right' and 'do it right now.' You may find it difficult to change eating habits if you are medicating emotions with overeating or under-eating and the neurochemical effects generated by these practices. Alcohol, sugary foods and over-breathing can shut down body awareness, and therefore help us manage anxiety. If your pelvic muscles are held in an ever-vigilant clench, it may be impossible for you to enjoy vigorous exercise. As you learn to regulate your autonomic nervous system with healthier practices and relationships, you will find it becomes much easier to enjoy eating well and exercising. (See 'Integrating the inner pharmacy.')

Remember to work in your personal learning zone, between anxiety and atrophy. Anxiety bathes our cells in cortisol and adrenaline and makes us less connected with our gut. But calm is not the whole answer. Failing to stimulate our nervous system with novelty and challenge means we will experience atrophy and deterioration. By expanding our personal learning zone with ongoing manageable challenge, we can groove new neural pathways and reweave the connection between gut and brain.

Exercise 52: Savoring

with thanks to Oriah Mountain Dreamer

Take an apple, grape, or another fruit you really enjoy for this exercise.

Focus on your fingertips, on the shape and weight of your hand, as you raise the fruit to your mouth, and let the tip of your tongue slide on the round, smooth firmness. Feel the spray of juice as your teeth pierce the skin, and enter the softness inside. Savour the smell and taste of it.

Taste in this fruit the loam of earth, the weeks of rain and sun, the ripening of the tree, the labor of the farmer, the touch of the fruit-picker, the truck on the highway, the ship on the sea, the transits of space and the interrelations of human and natural processes and relationships that bring this food to the table. Savour your gratitude for the web of connection.

Feel the fruit nourishing your body, transforming into energy that empowers the unfathomably intricate functioning of processes and systems within you. Taste the way this fruit nourishes the trillions of bacteria in your intestines that produce vitamins and neurochemicals and break down your food. Give thanks to the microbial garden within you.

Be with the immediate sensation of the food on your tongue, teeth and throat. Savour the ceremony.

Exercise 53: Mindful pooping

with thanks to Blandine Calais-Germain

The very idea of mindful pooping can incite a fit of giggles. Enjoy the silliness of this exercise!

As pooping has both voluntary and involuntary aspects, it is a portal into the autonomic nervous system. All too often, though, we miss the chance to tune into smooth muscle function; our pooping is a hurried act engaged with distaste and without much attention. Mindful pooping can be a way to calm and enliven your body, and forge a better gut-brain connection.

The rectum and anus are richly endowed with nerve endings, and simply tuning into your body feelings is a simple way to enjoy pooping. Your capacity to feel will build with practice, as sensation in a particular set of nerve endings changes and increases with focused attention. With tuning in can come memories of trauma, or a sense of shame. You may find your mind always skitters away from attending to this part of your body. As always, work in your personal learning zone.

The reflex action of pooping begins with a feeling of fullness in the rectum. The rectum is the segregated end of the large intestine. It begins approximately two inches up from the anal opening. The first step in mindful pooping is simply noticing that feeling of fullness.

When pooping is not immediately possible, we contract the muscles of the pelvic floor around the rectum, especially the puborectalis muscle. You can feel into this muscle by noticing your anus and then imagining going inside about an inch up the anal canal. A U-shaped muscle about 3/4-inch thick is anchored to both sides of the pubic bone in front, and comes back to form a sling around the anal canal. A contraction of this muscle draws the anus forward and flattens it. You can also stop poop by clenching the striated muscles of the external anal sphincter. This external sphincter of striated muscles is not just around the anal opening; it extends inside along the anal canal for about an inch. With the compression action of the puborectalis and anal sphincter muscles, the urge to poop is contained or disappears.

As the rectum fills more, the urge to poop comes again to the forefront of your consciousness. At some point you will be ready to poop immediately. Now the anal sphincter and the puborectalis muscles can relax. The angle of the anus shifts so the rectum and anus are almost aligned and the anal orifice can open. The smooth muscle of the rectal sleeve contracts and the expulsion reflex begins. Ahhhhh!

Often people habitually initiate pooping by pushing the thoracic diaphragm down to exert pressure on the rectum and anus. It is good to postpone this diaphragmatic push and just observe sensations. When the rectum functions normally, the smooth muscle narrows and shortens, which should be enough to expel the poop without any forcing action from the diaphragm. The rectum loses its muscular tone if diaphragmatic pushing is used habitually.

If you feel the need for some extra assistance, you can draw your navel toward your spine and then push it out again, over and over. This gives your digestive system a nice massage without the problematic downward diaphragmatic push that distends the anus and can cause hemorrhoids.

Just by paying attention to your body over a period of time, you will gradually reduce the need for any diaphragmatic pushing. The smooth muscle of the rectum will respond to your attention by regaining tonicity and doing its work.

This work is much easier when the rectum is not forced into a kinked position by sitting. Anatomically, we are meant to squat while pooping. A squat stool or other means to elevate your feet while pooping can help relax the anal sphincters and unkink the rectum to relieve strain.

Before you send your poop out into the world, take a few moments to notice the color, texture and smell. You can get much information about your physical and emotional health and wellbeing from your poop. Give thanks!

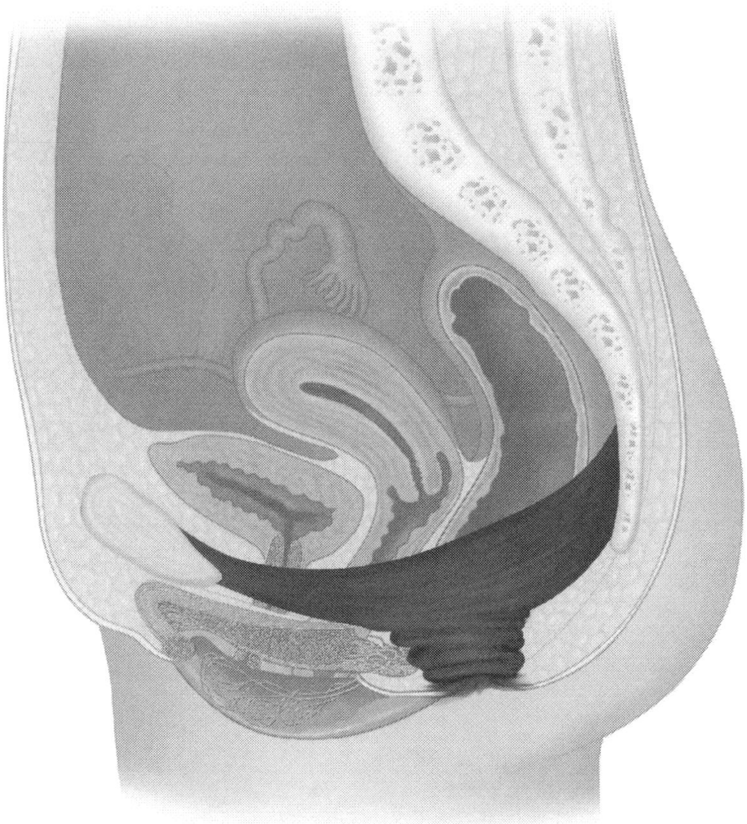

Figure 9: Pelvic diaphragm and anal sphincters

Integrating the Inner Pharmacy

A picture of the nervous system that shows brain, spinal cord and nerve fibers only tells part of the story. Also integral to nervous system function are hundreds of agents that function in our inner neurochemical environment—what I call the 'Inner Pharmacy.' Neurotransmitters and hormones act as chemical messengers that convey information between and among brain cells and body tissues, organs and functions. These chemical messengers are stimulated and inhibited in response to the world around and within us. They simultaneously affect and are affected by our actions, moods and thoughts.

Neurotransmitters are substances released from the end of a nerve fiber to a receptor cell on another structure. Their effects tend to be more precise, immediate and local. Hormones are created in glands and circulate through the bloodstream—their effects tend to be more widespread and long-lasting. Some chemicals including adrenaline and serotonin act as both neurotransmitters and hormones.

This list is offered as a tiny sampling of the unimaginably intricate processes through which our inner chemistry affects our sexual function. We can see in these descriptions how sexual trauma and neglect can impact our body chemistry. Thankfully, we can see there are choices we can make to integrate the 'Inner Pharmacy,' so our actions, thoughts and environment all contribute to a neurochemistry that supports our journey to sexual wholeness.

Dopamine is a neurotransmitter that affects sexual excitement, motivation, focus, energy and delight. Engagement with passion in any activity (including exercise and sex) increases dopamine levels. Sexual fantasy and sexual goals create a dopamine spike. Stress, poor nutrition, sugar, caffeine, drugs and alcohol deplete dopamine. When dopamine and serotonin levels are high, sex hormone production increases. Elevated levels of oxytocin trigger dopamine release, and vice-versa.

Oxytocin is a hormone produced in the hypothalamus. It is associated with bonding, and feelings of love, contentment and bliss. It is elevated through touch, acts of kindness, and connection with animal friends. Oxytocin levels soar with orgasm.

PEA (Phenylethylamine). PEA is a neurotransmitter that is an endogenous amphetamine, associated with mental energy, euphoria and love. PEA levels increase with sexual anticipation, erotic fantasy, savouring romantic memories, and sexual role play. They also increase with exercise and orgasm. PEA also appears to induce acetylcholine release. Increases in PEA elevate dopamine and serotonin levels.

Serotonin is a neurotransmitter associated with satisfaction and happiness and the function of smooth muscles in the food tube and our genitals. Use of serotonin reuptake inhibitors (SSRIs) is linked to decreased interest in sex. Paradoxically, high serotonin levels are linked with sexual happiness, but decreased access to orgasm, while low levels of serotonin are linked with sexual responsiveness and more accessible orgasm.

Acetylcholine (ACh), the first neurotransmitter ever discovered, was originally described as 'vagus stuff' because it is released by stimulation of the vagus nerve. It plays many roles in the body. In the central nervous system, ACh is part of our attention system and affects our responsiveness to sensory stimulation. ACh is the neurotransmitter that transmits signals between motor nerves and skeletal muscles. It is a transmitter for both the sympathetic and parasympathetic nervous systems. It is involved in the muscular components of sexual response and orgasm, and it mediates lubrication and engorgement.

Endorphins ('endogenous morphine') are neurotransmitters that produce a feeling of euphoria. Laughter, pain, delicious food, vigorous exercise and sex all trigger the release of endorphins.

Stress Hormones and Neurotransmitters: Cortisol, adrenaline and noradrenaline are all part of sympathetic nervous system arousal. They increase focus, aliveness and sexual interest in the short term. These chemicals are vasoconstrictors and can inhibit genital engorgement. Chronic stress dysregulates the hypothalamus-pituitary-adrenal (HPA) axis and inhibits sex hormone production (among other effects).

Prostaglandins are vasodilators that mediate engorgement and erection of genital tissues and help regulate the contraction of smooth muscle tissue at orgasm.

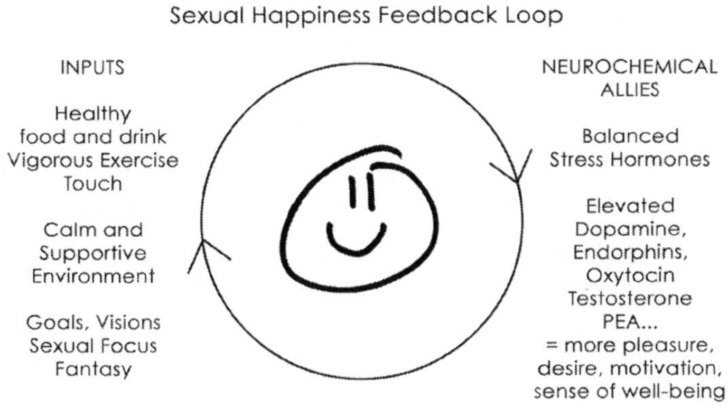

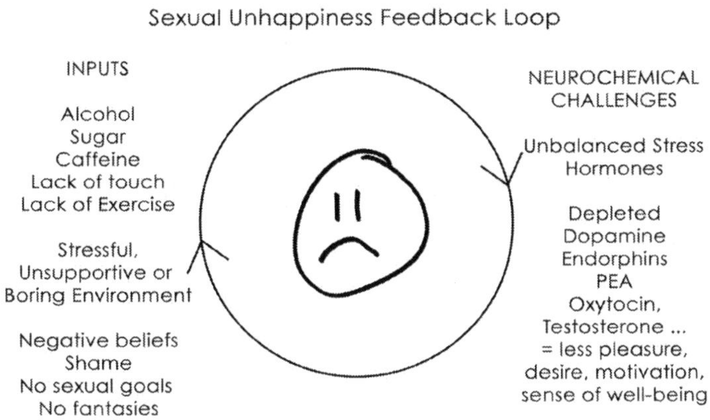

Figure 10: Integrating the inner pharmacy

In figure 10 we can see how behavior, thoughts, actions, environment and neurochemistry create a feedback loop. Choices that support sexual happiness in body, mind and environment trigger neurochemical effects that further support us in making more choices for sexual happiness. Choices that trigger sexual unhappiness in body, mind and environment initiate neurochemical effects that make happier choices more difficult. *We can intervene at any place in these feedback loops to create positive change.* Small steps like creating sexual goals, sharing more hugs, or choosing to drink less coffee (for examples) will generate neurochemical effects that support positive change, and greater sexual happiness.

Leptin is another one of many hormones that are crucial to sexual function. Low body fat, caloric deficits and excess exercise cause leptin levels to plummet, dysregulating the HPA axis and inhibiting sex hormone production (among other effects).

Sex Hormones: Androgens and estrogens affect sexual characteristics, behavior, fertility, desire and genital arousal. **Testosterone** is a primary driver of lust in both men and women. Testosterone levels can be boosted by vigorous exercise. **Estrogen** is the hormone primarily responsible for vaginal lubrication. Chronic stress inhibits hormone production. Sexual activities (including sexual thoughts and masturbation) boost levels of sex hormones. **DHEA** is a steroid hormone (androgen) that amplifies sex drive, protects the immune system and promotes bone growth. It can be increased by meditation, vigorous exercise and stress-reduction. Alcohol decreases DHEA.

Ending Shame

One of the most tragic effects of sexual trauma and neglect is the emotional legacy of shame. A preoccupation with self-criticism, a sense of being contaminated, an inability to absorb the praise and regard of others—these feelings are common for people who are struggling with embodied trauma and neglect. The felt sense of shame is not the same as self-judgment; it often makes no sense to the person's cognitive mind that they should feel shame about being a victim of a sexual predator, rejected by a depressed mother, or oppressed by social stigmas they do not believe in. Trauma and neglect can leave people with a deep sense of powerlessness, isolation, and shame that is felt and held in the body. The physiology deeply impacted by sexual trauma and neglect includes cardiovascular, respiratory, digestive, musculoskeletal, neuroendocrine, and autonomic nervous system function, as described in previous chapters. Emotional states are embodied through all these functions. Embodied experiences of happiness, loving kindness, play and pleasure are powerful ways to unwind shame from our cells.

Ending shame is not just a personal struggle. We live in a culture that shames sexual feeling. Anyone whose desires deviate from sexual stereotypes, and whose bodies are different from gender stereotypes, can meet with terrible punishments. There is little accessible education on arousal and genital anatomy, and even less on how to empower choice and voice in erotic encounters. Despite the widespread incidence of sexual trauma and neglect, there is little cultural knowledge of how these experiences impact people's lives. Ending shame requires us to create a new culture that welcomes and cultivates the erotic, celebrates body shape and gender diversity, and understands the effects of sexual trauma and neglect. Transforming cultural paradigms for sexual identity and sexual expression are key to creating a context where experiences of happiness, loving kindness, play and pleasure can unfold.

Some of the exercises I describe in this chapter are aimed at generating new cognitive understandings and new culture, while others aim to initiate physical experiences that can erase and replace the shame that gets embedded in our bodies and souls.

ENDING SHAME ABOUT CHAOS OR RIGIDITY

Knowing the impact of trauma and neglect on the autonomic nervous system can help us understand our needs and reactions around sex, and help us foster understanding with others in our lives. It helps to reduce shame when we know, 'this is how people react physiologically,' and that *we cannot simply override autonomic nervous system reactions with our thoughts.* Sometimes we need to go flat emotionally, disengage, go numb, get mad, run away, self-soothe, self-stimulate—in order to feel safe. Understanding the science can reduce shame about habitual emotions and behaviors, even as we gain more choices about how we act and how we feel. When support people and intimates understand, they are sometimes better able to offer the environment of loving kindness we need in order to change.

Neuropsychiatrist Daniel Seigel draws a model for mental health based on the self-organization of living systems. Seigel notes that in natural systems large and small an absence of wellbeing shows up as rigidity, chaos, or both. Wellbeing shows up as flexible, dynamic self-organization. The harmony of wellbeing emerges in open, living systems, with relatively safe, nutrient-rich surroundings, when there are high levels of diversity in the elements present, and high levels of complex interconnections.

We can see how sexual systems function within ourselves, and observe dysfunction when our complexity is stifled. Rigidity means being shut down, stuck, habitual, dead, numb, or inflexible in our sexuality. Chaos can look like intrusive, addictive, obsessive sex. When erotic feeling is unsafe, wounded, starved, covered up, repressed, ignored and impaired, it often leads to some form of rigidity and / or chaos. Rather than feeling shame about how rigidity and chaos show up in our erotic lives and relationships, we can compassionately notice these properties of a dysfunctional system. We are not rigid or chaotic people; we are identifying places where our sexual system needs more nutrients, more protection, more diversity or more interconnection to function in ways that foster our flourishing.

We can see how sexual systems function—and fail to function—on the macro level when we observe the culture of sexuality in which we swim. Where differences are disallowed or segregated, we see rigidity and chaos. Can we imagine and create the diverse, nutrient-rich surroundings we need for our personal erotic wellbeing?

Exercise 54: Identifying wellness and inviting change

How do rigidity and/or chaos show up in you, in your erotic life, and in the world around you? What does this feel like in your body?

What does sexual wellness mean to you? How does it contrast with rigidity and chaos? What can you do to create wellness in your own life, and in the world? Siegel notes that healthy natural systems are:

- **Flexible,**
- **Adaptive** and
- **Coherent**. They have
- **Energy** and
- fluid **Stability.**

Can you relate these words to your erotic life? Use the table on the next page to develop a vision of sexual wellness and identify places you want to invite change.

actions, feelings, visions or memories of **Rigidity**	actions, feelings, visions or memories of **Chaos**	actions, feelings, visions or memories of **Wellness**

ENDING BODY SHAME

My client Lisa is a young woman whose body seems, from the outside, to perfectly match the cultural ideal of a slender, fit, smooth and youthful woman. But Lisa *experiences* her body as scrawny, underdeveloped and undesirable. While she's trying to enjoy making love with her partner, her passion keeps being overwhelmed by her body shame. I have worked with plus-sized people who are confident and celebratory in their bodies, and others whose spirits seem crushed by adipose tissue. Aging leads some on a journey of unfolding of erotic joy, while demeaning cultural stereotypes keep others from ever getting naked. What makes the difference? How do we end body shame? It won't happen through adherence to exercise regimes, diets and plastic surgeries that offer everyone access to 'perfect' bodies! Instead we may need to go on a strict diet of avoiding engagement with popular culture and its body-shaming iconography. We need to make new culture. We need to create images, including sexual images, of people like ourselves, so that people with diverse bodies and sexualities are represented, honored and celebrated—in all sizes, shapes and ethnicities, and inclusive of disabled people as well as non-disabled. I believe that the shaming environment of popular culture is transformed when we work and play to change our physiological receptivity to demeaning stereotypes.

What was helpful for Lisa was coaching and practice in feeling her body from the inside. She had to link up practice being aware of body sensation with practice in boundary-setting, so she could stay present with her desires during a sexual experience. We moved from practice with feeling and expressing 'Yes' and 'No' to a touch session she guided. Afterwards she wrote: "It was a big realization for me that I really DO know what my body wants, and what I need, in any given moment. Related to that, guiding your touch was scary, but not in a terrifying way. Using my voice, and connecting that to my body awareness, was really powerful for me—I can already see that is shifting things for me. I feel like a lot integrity has been restored."

When people are tuned in and present with their bodies, they feel integrity. They are at one with their body sensation and can know and express their yearnings and emotions. From this basis, the body is a source of joy. Cultural stereotypes lose their sting.

There is no simple linear pattern that means people must first get tuned in and present with their bodies, and only then engage in joyful erotic experiences. Learning comes in a feedback loop, building strength from both directions. Increasing our capacity for staying present with body sensation builds more capacity for joyful erotic experiences, and joyful erotic experiences assist us in building capacity to be present with body sensation. These learnings unfold simultaneously within us, in an unending evolution of pleasures.

Exercise 55: Breath connects

adapted from Thich Nhat Hanh

Breathing in, I know I am breathing in.
Breathing out, I know I am breathing out.

Breathing in, my breath is deep.
Breathing out, my breath is slow.

Breathing in, I am aware of my whole body.
Breathing out, I feel my body whole. Ahhhh.

Breathing in, I smile to my whole body.
Breathing out, I feel my body smile. Yummm.

Breathing in, I smile to my genitals.
Breathing out, I feel my genitals smile. Ohhhh.

Breathing in, I touch my genitals.
Breathing out, I feel my genitals respond. Mmmmm.

Breathing in, I feel joyful.
Breathing out, I am the source of peace and joy.

Exercise 56: Sexual feeling is as innocent as breath

In a culture that shames sexual feeling, many people learn to numb out pleasure and aliveness in the genitals and surrounding tissues. We are actually designed to experience sexual pleasure with each breath.

Breathing in, the lungs expand, pushing the abdominal organs down into the belly and the pelvic floor. The muscle fibers of the pelvic diaphragm slide apart, the tailbone tips up, the bones of the pelvis move slightly apart. Breathing out, the muscle fibers of the pelvic diaphragm slide together. The tailbone comes slightly forward, the bones of the pelvis come together slightly. The nerves in the nerve-rich area of the genitals are gently stimulated from the inside every time we breathe.

Erotic energy circulates with each breath to every cell when we stimulate the genital nerves with deep pelvic breath. Stress-breath confined to the upper chest fails to activate the pelvic diaphragm or stimulate these nerves. Constraint in the pelvic floor keeps our genitals physiologically frozen and entombed.

Cultural silences weave together with the abnegation of feeling that happens breath-by-breath, creating a zone of numbness that sexologists call the 'genital hole' (a phrase that originated with A.H. Almaas). Simply tuning into the body sensation (or lack of sensation) we feel with every breath helps us begin to fill the 'genital hole' with information and energy. Neural networks that have atrophied can come alive when we pay attention, and begin giving erotic energy an honored role in our bodies and our lives.

For people who have experienced trauma, numbing the genitals is a frequently-used survival strategy. Even decades later, genital awareness may be inaccessible without triggering trauma memories. As always, work in your learning zone.

Sexual feeling is as innocent as breath. Our genitals can continually generate life-force energy, bringing joy to all our relations.

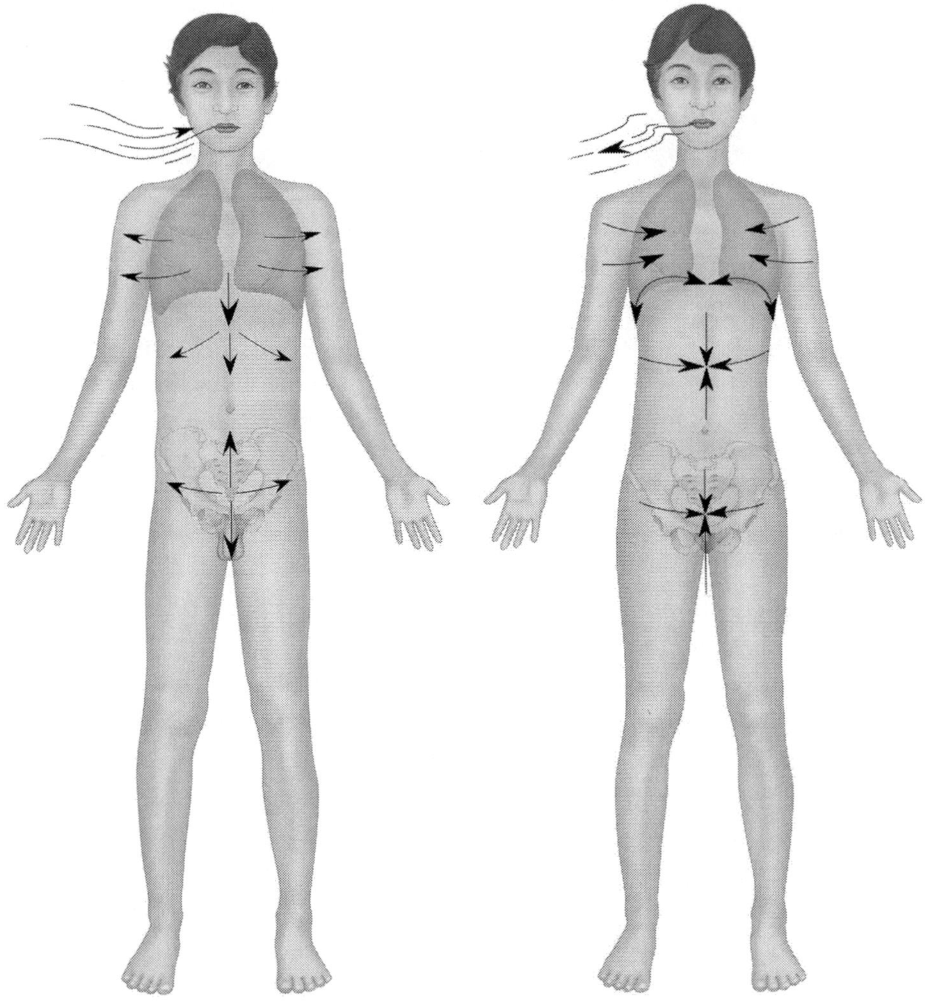

Figure 11: Breath stimulates the genitals

ENDING SHAME ABOUT GENITALS AND GENDER

Genital shame is common in a culture where education on what genitals really look like is so scarce. Whether I am teaching young people in schools or working with seniors, many are bedeviled by the question, 'Am I normal?' No one has taught them to see and celebrate the wondrous diversity of genital structures. What education there is comes through the surgically-altered, airbrushed images offered by the porn industry. So girls and women imagine that their long or asymmetrical inner labia are not beautiful. Boys think they need big circumcised penises to offer pleasure. Cosmetic genital alteration surgeries grow in popularity despite all the disadvantages, including decreased genital sensation, potential infection, tissue adhesions and scarring.

Based on external genital structure in infancy, we are assigned one of only two accepted sexes—and the gendering begins immediately, with a cascade of social and psychological consequences. Yet, as many as 75 per cent of the people I have seen in my practice as a somatic sex educator don't fit the sex and gender binary. Gender identity and gender expression sit alongside the biological complexity of sex, which includes genitals, sex chromosomes and hormones. So, it's no surprise that the limiting option of male or female is problematic for many people. The reductive approach of sex and gender assignment at birth based on external genital structure provides fertile ground for future genital shame.

Hormones, surgery, and other body modifications are vital to some transgender people. But no one should require genital surgery in order to claim a gender identity. No one of the infants born with 'ambiguous genitalia' should have gender assignment surgery imposed.

People who appear to fit neatly into male or female sex designations from the outside often harbor secret shame that something about their genitals, or their imaginal genitals, makes them 'abnormal.' But genitals are as different as faces. Just as there are many diverse and beautiful ways to have eyes, lips and noses, there are many diverse and beautiful ways to have erectile tissue, urethra and gonads.

Male and female are not opposites when it comes to genitals any more than we are opposites when it comes to faces. We have homologous genitals, as Emily Nagoski points out in her book, *Come As You Are*. In embryonic development, genital structures exist as bipotential tissue until around seven weeks, when they begin to diverge into structures we see as either vulvas or penises. Alice Roberts notes, "...the development of your external genitalia depends on whether or not you possess a Y chromosome, which will prompt your gonads to develop testes, which in turn produce testosterone. Without that masculinizing hormone, the unisex kit of parts develops into a female pattern…"

Genital and gender differences within and among us are part of the exuberant diversity that characterizes living systems. Vulvas and penises differ greatly in size and shape. In atypical (but still 'normal') development, these tissues develop differently yet, into genitals that are not readily identifiable as vulvas or penises. (These are differences that *normally* occur within populations.) There are also many diverse and beautiful ways to have transgender genitals—non-surgical, pre-surgical and post-surgical.

Imagine a world where everyone's genitals are celebrated as beautiful in their unique configurations. No child is assigned a gender based on genital structure. No child is hurt or shamed or filled with fear.

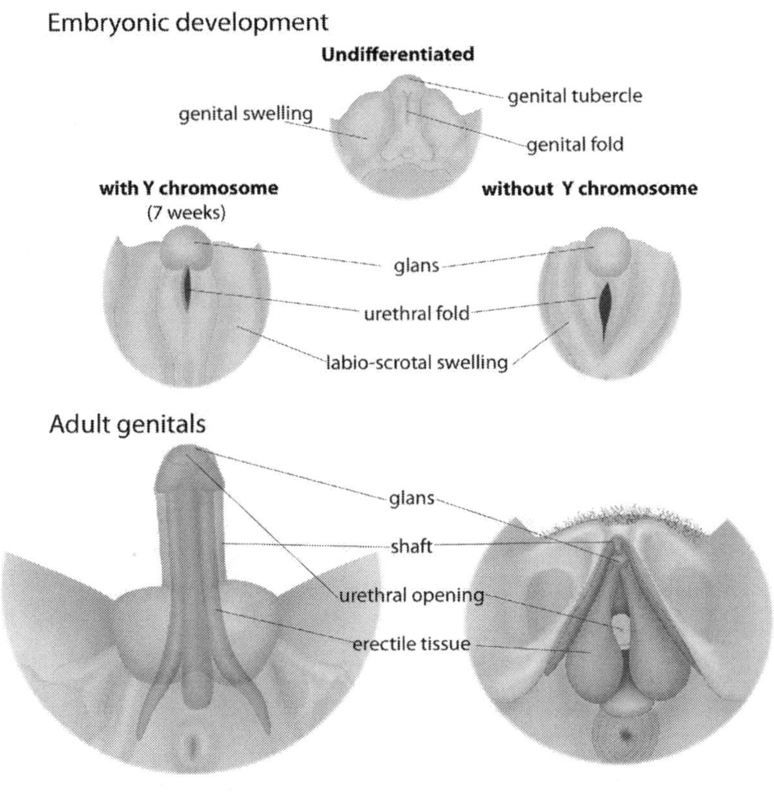

Figure 12: Homologous genital structures

Exercise 57: Mapping homologous genital structures

Relate the diagrams on the previous page to your own genitals. The table below lists additional facets of homologous genital structures. (For more detailed anatomical drawings, see my book *Erotic Massage for Healing and Pleasure.*)

Homologous Genital Structures	
Clitoral Glans	Glans of Penis
Clitoral Shaft	Corpus Spongiosum
Clitoral Hood	Foreskin
Legs of Clitoris	Crus Penis
Vestibular Bulbs	Corpus Cavernosum
Outer Labia	Scrotum
Ovaries	Testes
Urethral Sponge	Prostate
Vulvovaginal Glands	Bulbouretheral Glands
Fourchette	Frenulum
Inner labia	Inner foreskin
Urogenital slit	Raphe

Exercise 58: Genital meanings

adapted from Kate Bornstein, My Gender Workbook

Take one or more of these three questions. Devote ten minutes to writing down a series of answers. Free write without censoring yourself. Allow social, physical and personal meanings and images to mix together. If you run out of words, keep writing anyway. Try writing with your non-dominant hand as well as your usual hand.

What is a Penis?

What is a Vulva?

Why do we think we have one or the other?

UNDERSTANDING SEXUAL REFLEXES

Many sexual assault survivors experience physical pain and emotional horror during the trauma. For some, the experience of sexual violence can also include reflexive sexual arousal mixed with fear. This involuntary experience of sexual arousal is not pleasurable. It is the opposite of authentic pleasure when, in the middle of an act of terrible violation, a person being raped experiences an orgasm. It is the opposite of authentic pleasure when coercion includes seduction. But due to a lack of knowledge about sexual reflexes, there is immense shame surrounding the experience of physiological arousal during acts of sexual violence, and psychological bonding with an abuser during chronic trauma. Survivors tell me they feel guilt and shame about their physiological responses. They are further traumatized by being made to wonder if they 'secretly wanted' the violation or if they 'deserved' it. Police and courts may further shame them.

People also feel guilt and shame about not feeling arousal in situations where they most want to feel it. Sometimes with a caring, educated partner who engages in all the best practices, arousal and orgasm remain inaccessible. By understanding the physiology of sexual reflexes, we can end all this unnecessary shame.

Experiences of sexual arousal are *not* expressions of pleasure or consent—they are complex involuntary responses to diverse stimuli. As shown in Fugure 13, sexual response includes visceral and muscle reflexes plus reflex feeling-states and brain-states. Like sticking a finger down one's throat can produce a gag reflex, certain kinds of stimulation can produce arousal and orgasm. Shifts in the complex operations of any one of the contributing stimuli, and the dance between them, can make arousal inaccessible and derail orgasm, or trigger arousal and orgasm when it is unwanted and unenjoyed.

We can receive all the 'right' touch and not feel arousal because our mental attention is unfocused or our body is too stressed or too bored. We can receive terribly wrong touch and have an orgasm because our attention is riveted, and our sympathetic nervous system hyperactivated by fear

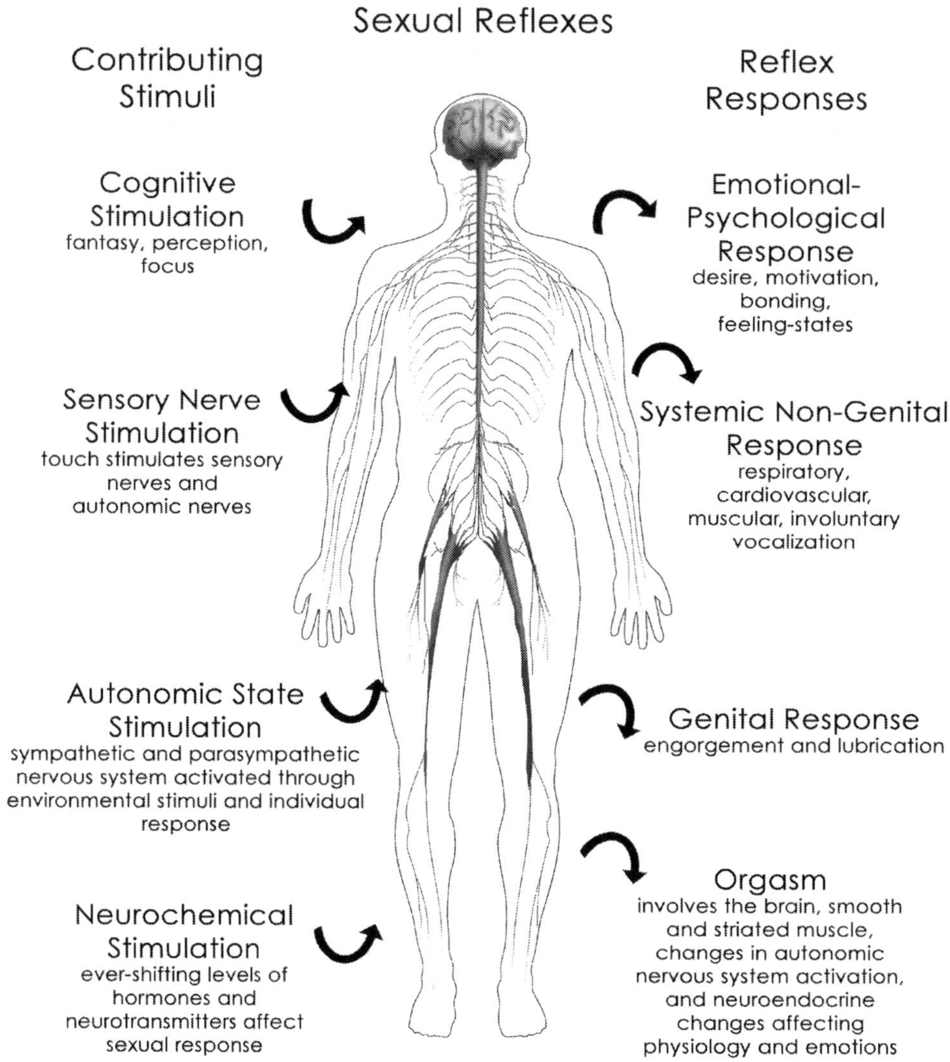

Figure 13: Sexual reflexes

Stimulation of one or more aspects of the nervous system can result in one or more of the reflex responses. Various contributing stimuli interact with each other, and this can trigger or disrupt reflex responses. Involuntary reflex responses are subject to learning.

For genital engorgement to happen, the parasympathetic nervous system needs to be activated so autonomic nerves dilate blood vessels in genital tissues. We can experience orgasm without genital engorgement. Or we can have a genital arousal response without ever cognitively perceiving ourselves as being aroused. Electroejaculation, carried out under a general anesthetic, reliably results in contraction of the pelvic muscles and ejaculation. People with Persistent Genital Arousal Disorder suffer from unwanted, relentless, and unprovoked genital arousal, unrelated to any feelings of sexual desire. Causes include sensory nerve entrapment and neuroendocrine stimulation. Other people want desperately to feel arousal but cannot. Causes include sensory nerve damage and cognitive blocks. The involuntary reflex responses of sexual arousal are not limited to the physical realm. Sexual arousal can also generate a neurochemically induced emotional bond with someone we cognitively dislike—a reflexive reaction.

Exercises like those in this book help us shift sexual arousal from the realm of involuntary reflex. Sexual reflexes are subject to learning. We can learn to cultivate and consciously stimulate the various aspects of the nervous system that contribute to sexual experience, and better integrate their functioning. We can engage and heal the whole arousal system: body, mind, spirit and emotions. An orgasm can be more than a genital sneeze; it can be an ecstatic alchemy.

Even with lofty goals and advanced practices, we need not undervalue the potential joys of our reflex responses. Ending shame about the diverse aspects of sexuality and living a commitment to loving kindness to ourselves and others, we can cultivate reflexive *and* expanded experiences of sexual arousal and orgasm.

Cognitive stimulation can be integrated and enhanced as we learn to pay attention to body sensation, integrate brain and body, gain conscious choice in autonomic nervous system state regulation, accept our desires, and cultivate our erotic imaginations.

Sensory nerve stimulation is integrated and enhanced as we learn to touch in more diverse and knowledgeable ways. We can also grow in our cognitive capacity to focus on the pleasure of sensory nerve stimulation. We can use touch to help regulate autonomic nervous system function and neuroendocrine function.

Autonomic state stimulation can be consciously engaged through various portals including breath, imagination, changing the environment, and physical stimulation of autonomic nerves. We can grow our capacity to feel deeply in very relaxed states, without falling asleep or becoming bored (expanding capacity of the parasympathetic nervous system) and to feel deeply in excited and highly aroused states, without being derailed by agitated hyperarousal (expanding capacity of the sympathetic nervous system). Expanded autonomic nervous system capacity increases our access to sexual arousal and orgasm when we cognitively link body sensation with sexual practice.

Neuroendocrine stimulation can be consciously engaged in various ways including touch, mindful movement, bold sensation and vigorous activity (see 'Integrating the Inner Pharmacy'). This in turn can affect our mood, willingness and readiness to feel sexual arousal and orgasm. We can consciously cultivate affection for pleasure partners, and understand how we chemically create or undo emotional bonds with people we don't like.

Exercise 59: From SOUP to NUTS

This exercise is helpful for feeling sexual arousal through both branches of the autonomic nervous system simultaneously.

We can reliably engage the parasympathetic nervous system when we mix ingredients with the handy acronym of SOUP.

S afety
O penness
U nderstanding
P leasant touch

Ingredients that reliably engage the sympathetic nervous system have the handy acronym of NUTS.*

* acronym was coined by the Montreal Center for Studies on Human Stress

N ovelty
U npredictability
T hreat
S ense of being out of control

Reflect on these acronyms in relation to your sexual practices (or the absence thereof). Create a self-pleasure experience that will simultaneously engage something from the 'SOUP' aspect of human experience and something from the 'NUTS' aspect. Play within your limits, while challenging yourself to expand them.

For a more challenging version of this exercise, create a 'SOUP to NUTS' role-play scenario with a partner.

Exercise 60: Engaging your body while watching porn and self-pleasuring

with thanks to Joseph Kramer who has developed extensive teachings for mindful porn-watching. This section is based on his work.

The practice of mindfully engaging with pornography helps grow links between cognitive processes and your autonomic nervous system. Notice—and make love—to your habits, gently coaxing your mind and body out of their neural grooves.

First, find porn that feels arousing for you, letting go of shame. (Watch your shame as it arises from the standpoint of the 'compassionate witness.' Get the collage you made of the compassionate witness and have it near you for this exercise.)

Just watch for a while, enjoying cognitive stimulation without sensory nerve stimulation. Then turn the porn off and physically stimulate your skin and genitals. Track your arousal levels as they drop or increase. Go back to porn watching without touch, and then back to touch without porn watching, simply noticing the stimulation of your arousal system.

If you are a habitual porn watcher, notice the ways you usually relate physically to pornography. Notice any contraction of muscles, the postures you assume, the ways you habitually breathe and touch yourself. Try doing something a little bit differently.

Possibilities include:

- Change position. Watch while standing, sitting, lying down and dancing. Move from one position to another.
- Go back and forth between tracking what is happening on screen, and what is happening in your body.
- Make noise! Sing, moan, grunt, call out words. Talk dirty.
- Breathe in rhythm with your movements. Try exploring the effects of faster breath and slower breath.
- Notice whether more engagement with the porn or more engagement with body sensation increases your arousal level.

ENDING SHAME ABOUT DESIRES

We need to give our whole-hearted approval to any and all desires that don't involve non-consensual touch (for integrating desires for non-consensual interactions see below). Having a desire doesn't mean you want to act on it now. But you might want to explore it sometime. So often, people shut down their desires before they even enter conscious awareness, because desire is yearning for something we don't yet have. Desire gives our lives impulse, color, energy and motion. If we are afraid of change (and we all are to some degree!) we will be afraid of our desires. Notice if your feeling in this exploration is 'I'm awake and alive with excitement' or 'I'm too scared to move because of fear.' Dial your engagement up or down so that you are playing in your learning zone.

Desires can reveal our differences. People in our support circle or people in the dominant culture might tell us that our desires make us bad, wrong, sick or illegal. The social consequences of expressing or acting on desires are real. We are raised in a culture shaped by centuries of sexual repression. Violence and hatred is directed at sexual minorities. Women have been oppressed, objectified and prohibited from free sexual expression. Transgression of cultural norms for sexual expression and gender identity can generate diverse punishments. Yet even though we may weigh potential punishments and choose not to act on or express our desires, I believe we need to feel into them, acknowledge them and give them some shameless form of expression (even if only in an abstract picture that can safely remind us of what we want). We may find it is a fear of suffering, rather than actual suffering, that keeps us small.

Our capacity for joy often expands with our capacity to challenge cultural norms that prohibit and inhibit our desires. I have written a whole book celebrating the joys of same-sex sexual desires and the differences they signal in contemporary culture (*Orientation: Mapping Queer Meanings*). Desires can lead us from the suffocating prison of ordinary life to an exciting engagement with love and community.

Desires hurt when we think that having these desires or acting on our desires makes us superior or inferior people. Desires are paths we can take to expand our lives and our sense of wholeness. Not getting what we want doesn't make us better or worse than getting what we want.

Sometimes people shut down their desires before they reach the level of conscious awareness because desires make us so vulnerable. Not getting our desires met can leave us feeling terribly sad, jealous, rejected, wounded and alone. We have to feel brave enough, and resourced enough, to survive the suffering of unmet desires in order to feel our desires deeply, and then ask for what we want. Before we ask, we often need to have a sense of safety with the person or community we express our desires to. If the answer is No, will we still be cared for? Will we be shamed? We can all contribute to creating social environments where people feel safe enough to feel into their vulnerability and ask for what they want. This requires that those hearing an expression of desire will receive it gladly, and not as a demand. My friend and mentor Dr. Liam Captain Snowdon often prefaces his requests by saying, 'Your No is as sexy as your Yes!'

Desires hurt when they are expressed in the form of criticisms or entitlements.

Exercise 61: Lust list

with thanks to Dr. Liam Captain Snowdon who developed this exercise and the following exercise

Take just three minutes and quickly list twenty sensual and erotic things you would like to do someday. If it's strong for you, you can list the same thing twenty times.

Exercise 62: Desire interview

Interview yourself or do this with a partner. Be an investigative journalist to your desire. Take one thing from your lust list and write a paragraph about it. Who or what with? What will you do? Where will you be? What is the time, temperature and texture of the event? What do you smell? What do you hear? What do you see? What do you feel in your body? Take time to imagine and savour. Don't ask why. Ask what, where, who, when and how.

Exercise 63: Desire research

Having identified an important desire with the 'Lust list' and 'Desire interview,' do some 'Desire research.' Look for erotic images. Read erotica written by people who had similar desires. Watch porn. Find someone you can talk with who has had related desires or experiences. Is there a website or book you can read? Is there an educator you can contact? Is there a group you can join? Is there a workshop you can take? Is there a way to role-play online? Take your desire seriously and spend time researching it. Know that you can always say 'No' to your own desire, or anyone else's desire, at any time. (ANY TIME, even in the middle of an erotic encounter. ANY TIME.)

FANTASIES, DESIRES AND GOALS

This chapter owes much to the folks at Pleasure Mechanics, who create wonderful resources for erotic learning.

In the description of sexual reflexes at the-beginning of this chapter, it is important to note that thoughts, imaginations and perceptions that happen in the cerebral cortex act as vital nervous system stimulants. One of the simplest and most effective ways to reclaim a connection with erotic pleasure in the wake of trauma and neglect is to cultivate the erotic imagination. Fantasies can be much more than snippets of distracted erotic thoughts. Elaborated stories that evoke sensual pleasures can stimulate the nervous system and generate physiological arousal.

Yet people often eschew their fantasies, or use them sparingly, because they feel ashamed that their fantasies include people or other beings, practices, organs or orifices they would never want to interact with in the realm of reality. Ethics, communication and consent are essential in the realm of reality, but in the realm of fantasy we can honor all the archetypes that show up. Sometimes, for some of us, that will include unsafe sex, sex with people or other beings we aren't in a relationship with, forbidden pleasures, and violent, non-consensual sex. In the realm of fantasy, we can welcome and play with it all.

Let your fantasies be rich with sensual details—fantasize about smells, tastes, textures, colors and physical sensations. Try on different playmates and different settings. Try on different gender roles and dominance/submission roles for yourself. Notice that fantasy is a full-body experience—and savour your body's responses. By committing time to our fantasies, paying attention to any arousal they generate, and making them deeper, richer and more fully developed, we are building our brain maps and integrating neural networks.

Exercise 64: Cultivate fantasy: Make up a story from an erotic image

Searching images, you can probably find a photograph of something you find erotic on the Internet. Find an image of something or someone that sparks a little spike of arousal in your body. Drink in the details of the image, then close your eyes and imagine with all your senses. What do you see, hear, smell, feel, and taste in this scenario? What in the setting is sexy? Make up a story around the image. What would you like to do with the being or object in the image? What details would you change to make it even sexier?

Make a scrapbook or electronic scrapbook of erotic images from the Internet that you can turn to when you want to stimulate your arousal.

Exercise 65: Cultivate fantasy: Fantasy doorways meditation

Explore finding a doorway to a surprising fantasy that is just right for you, and allowing it to unfold. Please find this guided "Fantasy doorways' meditation online. You can download the MP3 audiofile for free at erospirit.ca/gifts. After listening to the meditation, take time to write about what you experienced, thought or felt.

CORE EROTIC THEME

Sometimes fantasies point to things we would like to bring into our lives. Other fantasies point to practices that would be dangerous, destructive or hurtful if acted upon in real life. Such fantasies are common. Many refer to archetypes we will explore in the next exercises.

The erotic imagination is unruly, rarely following cultural scripts and gender-based prescriptions about what we should want to do with whom. Psychologist Jack Morin describes how our 'core erotic theme' (CET) often involves taking the difficult material of our early life and turning it into pleasure, using "old wounds and conflicts as aphrodisiacs." So someone who has been neglected and unwanted as a child might overcome such obstacles through fantasies and experiences of being infinitely desirable. People who have been subjected to sexual violence as children might have a CET involving domination and surrender. People who have had too much responsibility in their youth might feel chosen by fantasies and scenarios of anonymous sex in which their feelings and competencies don't matter. These are just simplified examples and by no means represent all responses.

By examining the persistent fantasies that fuel our erotic turn-ons, we gain more choice in how our CET manifests in our lives. A CET of surrender, unacknowledged and unscrutinized, might pull us into relationships where we are bullied. A CET of being irresistibly desirable might leave us feeling unloved and unappreciated in ordinary human relationships.

Exercise 66: Fantasy to desire

Look for common themes, activities or energies that fuel your fantasies. Pay attention to what parts of your fantasies are most powerful and meaningful to you. Do you notice a CET emerging? Notice all the people, animals, objects and actions in your fantasy—and consider how all of them may be aspects of you. Is there an exciting element in this fantasy that you really want to explore in real life? Are there ways the theme in this fantasy has explored you?

How does fantasy translate to real-life desire? Tuning in to the real-life desires you can tease out of your fantasies is fun. It can also help to undo a sense of compulsively choosing forms of erotic expression that leave us feeling less than whole, or relationship roles we don't want. On the other hand, there is no necessary progression from fantasy to desire. Sometimes a fantasy is just a fantasy, and that is a wonderful thing too.

Free-write about your fantasy and desire. Use these prompts to tease out the differences.

I fantasize about:
I feel excited when:
I want more:
Images of ________ turn me on.
I'd like to:

Exercise 67: Desire to goal setting

Your fantasy might be to offer erotic massage to a series of strangers on a beach in a tropical paradise. Looking at what's really hot for you in this fantasy, you might identify a desire to study and practice erotic massage. A goal might be to research and attend a weekend massage course in your area by February 14. Or you might get a copy of my book *Erotic Massage for Healing and Pleasure.*

In your fantasy five brutal cops ravish you. When you look at this, and feel what is hot, you might find a desire to explore the energy of power and surrender in consensual sex play with a caring friend. A specific goal might be to discuss your desire with a potential playmate by May 1st.

You have great resources in your fantasies, and in your 'Lust list.' You can decide to keep all these in the realm of cognitive stimulation, or you can turn some of these into goals—on your own or involving other people. You get to decide what is right for you, knowing you can change your mind at any time. (Yes, ANY TIME. Even in the middle of an agreed-upon sexual exchange. ANY TIME!!)

My desire is to:____.

My specific goal is to ________________________________ by ________ (date).

SHADOW PLAY

'Shadow' is a psychological concept that refers to the unconscious contents of mind and culture. Shadow is what we forget and deny. In erotic life, all ways of being cast shadows—those we judge as 'good' as much as those we judge as 'bad.' We can become more whole, and more intentional, by dialoging with our erotic shadows. Shadow energy can be passionate and strongly creative, and it is sometimes exaggerated and destructive.

We can recognize shadows in qualities we especially dislike or see as unattainably wonderful in others. Is there an 'other' way of being or thinking that you define as evil, ugly or wrong? Is there an 'other' way of being or behaving that seems pure and beautiful? Now look at how your judgments of either 'good' or 'bad'—but different from you—can show up in various parts of you and your erotic life. Look for the gold in the shadow you castigate; look for what is unhelpful in what you worship. Shadows are parts of us, sometimes parts that need to be listened to, and sometimes parts that need to be disregarded. Shadows are potential allies we can dance with, resist, or embrace.

Shadow play is about finding balance, and working with density, so that we can explore and integrate nuances instead of seeking clear delineations between good and evil, self and not-self. When we take the heroic journey out of the ordinary world into the world of sexual wholeness, we are bound to meet and dance with shadows.

We all have an idea of what sexual depravity is. In erotic life, depravity claims space. It can be expressed in pathologies and exorcised with self-righteousness. Or depravity can find subtle expressions and finely-articulated niches, in costume, erotic play, art, sexual culture. Our worst nightmares lead us deep inside. Given time and attention, they can nourish the soul.

We all have an idea of sexual innocence, perhaps a sense of 'original innocence' from which we are wrenched away by sex. All too often, survivors of trauma and neglect see themselves as irrevocably broken—their original innocence projected onto the trusting child they once were. But shadow play allows us to recuperate our innocence for the present moment. We can practice innocently open-hearted ways of meeting inner and outer worlds with optimism and trust.

Shadow play may reveal that both wide-eyed innocence and genuine depravity are included within us. Accepting this, we can honor the polymorphous perversity that curiously belongs to the deepest innocence. We can see how depravity and innocence are not so opposite, and understand how purity of heart, playfulness, trust and openness can be pathways to defilement, self-acceptance, and integration of shadows.

Exercise 68: Mirror meditation: 'I love you'

Find a picture in a magazine or on the Internet (or in your photo album) to represent a beloved person or quality that feels infinitely desirable and out of reach. Tape it to your mirror. What do you see? Name the qualities of the person or being that you yearn for. Now look at your own image in the mirror. Breathe those qualities into your body. Notice how they are received. Are there eager receptors for these qualities within you? Are those very qualities already there?

Offer yourself appreciation. Look at your outer shell and name what you see that is beautiful. Is there kindness, gentleness, power, passion in your face or posture? Notice that behind the skin there are the infinitely intricate processes of blood circulation, cell division, neuronal firing.... Offer your body your heartfelt appreciation. Fill it with your care, your witnessing of what is amazing and beautiful.

Let your gaze go back to the picture and feel your attraction to the qualities it represents. Offer your love to these qualities, saying 'I love you.' Let your gaze come back to your own eyes. 'I love you. I love you.'

Exercise 69: Be the monster

What are a few things about the exploration of sex that bring up fear for you? Name the monsters. (These could include fear of being shamed for sharing a desire, shame about trying something new and failing at it, disappointing your family, losing control, pain, relationship rupture, or being weird, insatiable, retraumatized, victimized.) Of the monsters that scare you, are there any that also bring that little shiver of arousal or curiosity? Imagine dressing up as that monster. What would your hair look like, how would you dress, what would you wear? Make a mask for the monster. Put it on and feel into how you can act like the monster. How would you behave? What would you sound like? How would you interact with others? How would you have sex? Practice moving while wearing the mask. Get sexy, in the way that's peculiar to this monster. Experiment with taking off the mask and putting it on.

ARCHETYPES

Archetypes are powerful, living symbols that link us to myth and history. Carl Jung describes them as "involuntary manifestations of unconscious processes," and "the thoughts that think you."

Archetypal characters that often populate the erotic imagination include Predator, Victim, Mother, Father, Child, Monster, Innocent, Teacher, Student, Bully, Youth, Virgin, Whore, Wild Thing, Soul Mate, Animal.

Big archetypal themes that are common in erotic fantasies include:

- Boundary transgression: offending cultural prescriptions on race, age, gender identity, sexual orientation, class, incest taboos
- Surrender
- Being forced to experience pleasure
- Defilement
- Being infinitely desirable, being desired by many
- Seduction
- Abduction
- Pursuit
- Punishment
- Anonymous sex
- Slow, tender sex
- Violent sex
- Rape
- Humiliation
- Group sex
- Gender Transformation
- Hidden Passion
- Secret Identity
- Forbidden Desire
- Overwhelming Passion
- True Love

The archetypal images and meanings we connect with through erotic fantasy ('the thoughts that think you') can represent mythic narratives and potentialities. They can be guides to our power to change our personal lives and the culture that surrounds us. Rather than interpreting and untangling the web of association with our analytical minds, we can use images, poetry, free writing and creative play to approach and integrate the multi-layered meanings of archetypes, and the journeys, tasks and attainments they invite.

Exercise 70: Feed your demons

with thanks to Melissa Bee

I have met many people who feel they are struggling with demons when it comes to sex. Sometimes people obsess over lovers they know are wrong for them. People can be haunted by pornography they viewed years ago, hated, and yet feel drawn to in fantasies again and again. Sometimes people find themselves playing the same role over and over in sexual relationships—and feel stuck being the teacher, aggressor or victim.

Tsultrim Allione, author and teacher in the Tibetan Buddhist lineage, describes our fears, obsessions, and addictions as parts of ourselves that have become 'demonic' by being split off, disowned, and struggled against. When we try to flee from demons, they pursue us. When we fight against them, they grow stronger. If we give them what they need, we can free ourselves. My colleague Mehdi Dervish and I have incorporated parts of Tsultrim's process for 'Feeding your demons' into shadow play explorations at our Intimacy Education workshops.

We begin with a meditation that helps us relax and dive into the erotic unconscious. We swim in a sea of potential demons and decide, from this open-hearted place, which demon we will work with. What demon is present in your current sexual dilemmas or fantasies? What demon seems to choose you?

1. Find the demon in your body.

2. Personify the demon and ask what it needs.

Visualize the demon and ask: "What is it that you want from me? What do you need? If you get what you need, how will you feel?"

3. Become the demon.

Become the demon, and answer the questions above. Feel the ache for what is missing. Feel what it would be like to really get what you need. Feel how you will feel when that happens.

4. Feed the demon.

Become yourself again. Reaching deep inside, feel yourself resourced by the earth that holds you, the water that circulates in and around you, the air you breathe, the inner fire that warms you. Know yourself as a channel that can tap into an endless reservoir of whatever the demon will feel when it gets what it needs. Channel this feeling through you into the demon. Keep feeding the demon, until its complete satisfaction is reached. When it is fully sated, allow the demon to disappear. Gradually return to ordinary consciousness.

5. Journal and draw.

Make notes and sketch images. You can keep using the writing prompt, 'I am the one who....'

Another Version:

Integrate your insights into a creative erotic ritual. You might have someone represent the demon and touch you in certain ways. You might play with your demon, play with having the demon become an ally, change places in the ritual.

ENDING SHAME

It is part of the legacy of chronic childhood trauma, oppression and neglect that we have never developed a core sense of 'okayness' (More on this in the chapter on 'Attachment Patterns.') If we didn't belong and feel cherished as children, we can become isolated, self-absorbed and self-critical. From this perspective, there is no end to the list of things we can feel ashamed about—even shame itself. People often cling to shame and negative self-judgments, fearing that only their most rigorous self-criticism will give them sufficient motivation to change. Yet their constant self-undermining leaves them off-balance, under-resourced, and unable to sustain meaningful change.

I believe that effective and lasting change can best emerge when we move *towards* pleasure, joy and goodness, with a foundation of self-understanding and self-acceptance. Caring witnesses, and our own inner compassionate witness, are important resources on this journey. We can learn to gently shift our perspective, so that we see all our thoughts, feelings and behaviors from the viewpoint of the compassionate witness. We can relate *to* feelings rather than *from* them, offering our shame detached and kind attention. At the same time, connection, pleasure and play can transform the core woundedness that shame expresses.

Exercise 71: Counsel the Shame

As a person who has experienced sexual shame, you are empowered with skills, knowledge and abilities that helped you survive. This means you have the ability to help others deal with their experience. How can people make the tragedy in their sexual lives into a meaningful source of information and energy? Imagine someone reaching out to you for counseling who is feeling shame. How would you guide them? What would you want them to feel? How can they mend?

Variation: Write a letter to a person who is feeling shame.

Powered by Pleasure

What do you prefer? Who do you want? Where is your pleasure? What makes you happy? What excites you? When do you feel most alive? Pleasure is an inner guide that empowers us to seek nourishment, companions and environments that fit our needs, where we can unfold our whole potential. This pleasure-seeking impulse is part of our cellular intelligence. An amoeba moves towards optimum temperatures; a nematode worm learns to avoid shock; a plant grows towards the light. We are built to seek conditions that support our flourishing and withdraw from stimuli that hurt or inhibit us. When we are forced to endure trauma, oppression and neglect, our inner guidance system is damaged. Our culture further skews our self-trust with messages that pleasure is essentially bad, sexual pleasure is especially wrong and depraved, and erotic energy must be controlled and repressed. We are trained to deny and denigrate sexual pleasures.

Recovery means learning to trust our personal pleasure-seeking impulse. In small ways, over and over, we can create conditions in which we cultivate awareness of our own true yearnings. Each time we choose pleasure, we learn to follow the inner Yes, and build the self-trust that that helps us discern more pleasures. Deepening our experience of joy and wellbeing, we are also learning to trust the inner No—to avoid harm, including self-harm, and to deflect what and who will inhibit us.

Exercise 72: Awakening the pleasure of touching

My mentor and colleague Betty Martin always begins her programs by guiding people to tune in to the pleasure in their skin.

Our nerve endings come alive when we fondle objects with mindful awareness. Let your mind sink into the pleasure of pure sensation. Take time to savour the pleasure of touching. Often we are so focused on a task we are doing, or focused on another person's pleasure, that we forget to notice and be guided by our own pleasure. Close your eyes and go outside of naming the object you are touching. Just focus on your sensual experience of the object. Notice your mind depart then bring it back. Focus on the pleasure of touching the object for no purpose other than your pleasure. Follow your inner Yes—tapping, poking, caressing. Glide your skin over surfaces, sinking into the pleasure. Let pleasure occupy your mind and heart.

Exercise 73: Body maps for mapping pleasure

There are two body maps to try: one to map contentment, and one to map excitement. Recall the difference between contented good feelings and excited good feelings that we explored previously.

For the first diagram, imagine or remember contented good feelings and notice your body sensations. Scan your body to track texture, temperature, vibration, movement impulse. Use colors and patterns to record body temperature, pressure, vibration, and sensation.

For the second diagram, imagine or remember excited good feelings and notice your body responses. Try to draw and map the feeling-states in your body. Use colors and patterns to record body temperature, pressure, vibration, and sensation.

Reflect on the unfamiliarity or familiarity of these feeling-states.

Variation: Imagine and practice saying Yes as a movement toward and into your pleasure. Imagine and practice saying No as a way of deflecting obstacles to your pleasure. Notice how it feels to affirm and defend your pleasure, and track this feeling on a Body Map.

Body Map: Contentment

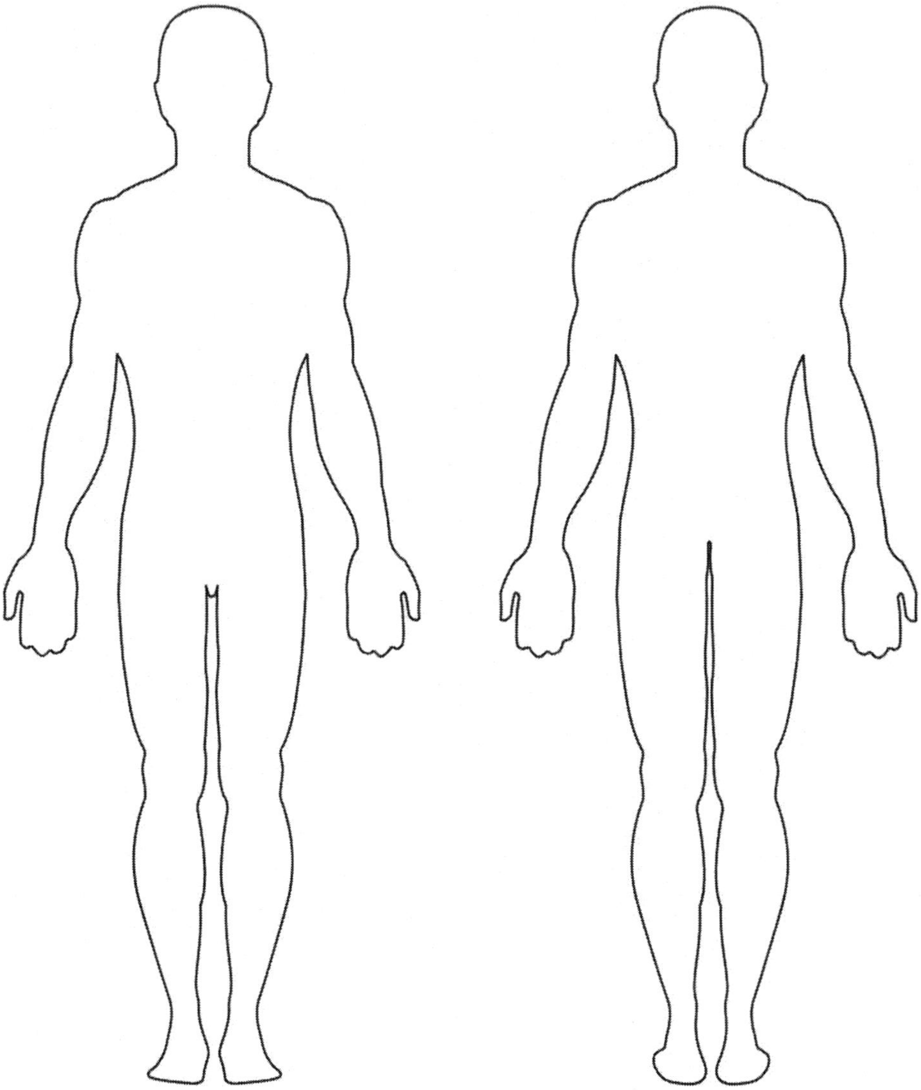

Body Map: Excitement

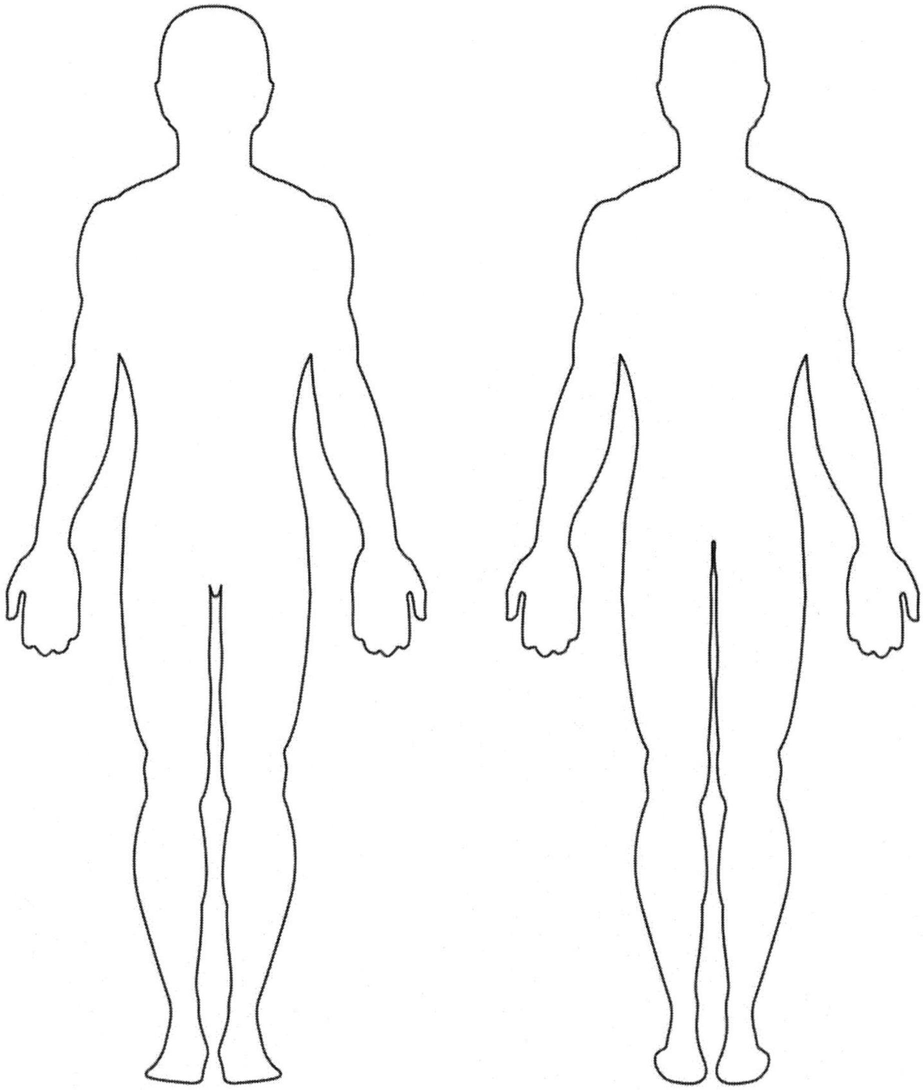

A DIET OF PLEASURE

What would be a diet of pleasure? Here I am using the word diet in its root sense, from Greek *diaita,* meaning 'manner of living.' People attempt to control their diet by self-denial. They castigate themselves as weak-willed and foolish for the pleasures they indulge in. They imagine that if they follow their pleasure they will end up eating mountains of sugary food, or having dangerous sex day and night.

It is true that our nervous system can become addicted to hyperstimulation. We can groove neural pathways that depend on intensity. This can show up in various ways for people sexually, with addiction to porn, to new or dangerous sexual experiences, or unwanted violent fantasy. With practice, we can become more sensitive to quiet and subtle pleasures, if we want to. But if noisy, high-intensity pleasures are what support your full thriving, by all means welcome and celebrate what works for you.

Look for the seeds of your authentic joy within your temporary pleasures. Ask, 'What is the true pleasure?' while trusting yourself and your desire. A passion for sugary donuts might suggest a yearning for the sweetness of life. An attachment to the pleasures of high-risk sex might lead you to recognize your desire to cultivate extraordinary connections with others, or to embody your power and independence. Porn addiction might mean you yearn for transcendent ecstasy.

There is no bad, but sometimes we choose maladaptive or substitutive pleasures, or pleasures that temporarily soothe but eventually harm us or others. With a willingness to attend to pleasure, and to let pleasure deepen, we are more likely to choose pleasures that support our living fully.

Exercise 74: Savoring peak erotic experiences

with thanks to Jack Morin

Take a deep breath, pause for a moment, and think about some special erotic experience, a heartfelt sexual pleasure you have enjoyed in your lifetime, whether alone or with others.... Enter the memory.... Find the taste, the sights, the sounds, the felt sensations in your body....Notice what you feel in your body. Notice your skin, your heartbeat and your breath. Savour every aspect of the memory awhile....10 seconds, 20 seconds.

Wonderful sexual experiences are inaccessible to some people. But for many, positive erotic experiences do manage to make it into long-term memory, where they become permanent resources we can tap into, again and again. These memories aren't the judgments we hold about what happened or the stories we tell about our experiences. They are physical sensations, called 'implicit memories.' The bad stuff is there too—the wash of terror or shame we felt during a negative sexual experience can well up unbidden and shape our current life. We can feel anxious, angry or turned off, even when we 'know' with the thinking mind that this is a different situation, with someone we *want* to explore and enjoy. But the good stuff is also there, alive and present.

People often don't access the pleasure of their peak erotic experiences because they judge them as shameful. Perhaps these experiences didn't happen with their spouse, or they involved some element of danger or transgression. But if we recall and savor peak erotic experiences, and mine the pleasure, it actually helps us neurologically build a bigger capacity for embodied joy.

GET STICKY FOR PLEASURE

According to neuropsychologist Rick Hanson, negative experiences are sticky. Our brain is like Velcro for negative experiences, and like Teflon for positive experiences. The brain has this negativity bias embedded in its structure, developed through millions of years of evolution. A physiological bias towards noticing and focusing on bad experiences helps us avoid danger. This bias helped our ancestors survive.

A general physiological bias towards focusing on the negative is expanded by difficult life experience. Infant experiences of cold detachment, or of being surrounded by chaos, get encoded in the autonomic nervous system and reflected in its vigilance. Heart, brain and body become biased towards fear and abandonment. Experiences of warmth and security help us become more open and optimistic. Psychiatrist Bessel van der Kolk notes, "If you feel safe and loved [as a child], your brain becomes specialized in exploration, play and cooperation...."

The ability to learn from bad experiences probably helped each of us survive some degree of trauma and distress. And it will always remain important to track real threats. However, if we fail to focus on and learn from pleasurable experiences, our *capacity* to experience pleasure is severely impaired.

We have already discussed how the brain is continually changing its structure in response to the energy and information flowing through it. The brain takes its shape from whatever the mind routinely rests upon. There are numerous biophysical mechanisms through which what we think and feel builds brain structure.

To name just four:

1. There is more blood flow to busy areas of the brain.
2. The synapses at the end of nerve fibers are formed and broken down moment-by-moment in ways that are activity-dependent. Neurons that fire together, wire together. Parts of the brain get more densely developed with increased activity. Dendritic spines on neurons rapidly change shape in ways that are influenced by multiple factors including stress.
3. Gene expression and resilience change in response to environmental factors.
4. Neurons alter their neurotransmitters with changing circumstances.

Over twenty mechanisms of neuroplasticity have been identified, and this research is just beginning.

The new scientific understanding of neuroplasticity has inspired a new approach to the treatment of chronic physical pain. This approach is also useful for addressing emotional pain and cultivating pleasure. Pain begins as a signal of an emergency. It brings an injury urgently to our awareness, so that we can do something to change the situation and relieve the pain. If changing the situation is not possible, pain has no useful function for the organism. But pain is quite likely to increase rather than diminish in this situation. When we *focus* on the pain, the area of our brain that is devoted to focusing on pain expands, and the pain can get bigger and unrelenting. Since neuroplasticity is the mechanism that produces chronic pain, using pain as a signal to consciously focus on something else is an effective treatment for chronic pain. It is also a great way to address habitual shame and obsessive attachments. Let the thought you *don't* want trigger you to choose a thought, image, or action that you *do* want—one that brings you pleasure.

Repeatedly noticing and savoring a broad spectrum of pleasures is the doorway to developing a reliable pleasure-seeking impulse within ourselves. Repeatedly savoring positive experiences past a critical threshold of 10-20 seconds gradually tunes the vigilance system of the brain to noticing pleasure. Our brain becomes increasingly sensitized to positive and pleasurable experiences, and gradually desensitized to the negative. We increase the ability to feel the sympathetic branch of the nervous system activation as excitement rather than distress, and the parasympathetic branch as contentment rather than apathy.

We can effect this change by *noticing* pleasurable experiences, even in small ways. Then, we need to savour them. Stay with your pleasure, slow it down, and enrich it with your attention and commitment. *Notice* what you are feeling in your body and soul. Absorb it. Breathe it in. In this way we gradually change the structure of the brain and develop a neurological allegiance to authentic pleasure.

Cultivate erotic joy

We literally change our mind and body when we cultivate joy through the practice of pleasure. Hanson suggests three steps:

Observe. Learn to be with all that is, within and without. Practice mindful awareness.

Pull weeds. Release/reduce negative thoughts.

Plant flowers. Choose pleasure in small and large ways. Practice and savour pleasure.

We can each cultivate the garden of our erotic wellbeing in this way.

1) **Observe** yourself and your unique erotic ecosystem with compassionate kindness. Your personal history, inborn tendencies, and the different natural and human communities you live in shape the garden of your erotic wellbeing. Notice what gives you erotic pleasure in small and large ways: physical, emotional, mental and spiritual. Notice your inner, outer and emerging resources. Notice what you are grateful for.

2) **Pull weeds** by noticing your shame, self-judgment, negative thoughts about yourself and your body, relationships (or the absence of relationship), access (or lack of access) to orgasm, use (or lack of use) of toys, porn, fantasy. 'Pulling weeds' doesn't mean you need to lose weight, get a better relationship, have bigger orgasms, and stop using porn. Our *negative thoughts* are the weeds in our erotic garden. It is our *shame* about erotic life that diminishes us, rather than any aspect of our erotic life itself. Pull weeds by gently observing your negative self-judgments and releasing them with loving kindness, refocusing on what is positive and pleasurable now.

3) **Plant** what you want to harvest. Each person's garden can produce beautiful nourishing foods of pleasure. We can plant things like lettuce seeds that make food in weeks and apple seeds that take many years to fruit. Both the fast-growing and slow-growing foods are pleasurable and beautiful. So, plant more joyful and pleasurable erotic practices and cultivate

rich, abiding erotic relationships with guidance from this book and others. Dream into what you want for yourself and your erotic life, plant the seeds, and provide, as best you can, the conditions for your vision to flourish. Be patient and be companioned by pleasure. Savoring the process will best prepare you for the harvesting the ripe fruit.

At the right pace

We have to foster our capacity for pleasure and positive emotions at a pace that is right for us. Every person is different. With each person there will be a different answer to the question: 'How can I have experiences that support me in building my sexual confidence, self-compassion and joy?' People who are in distress may need to stay there, and allow their grief to unfold in its own time. The practice of pleasure does not mean shutting down negative emotions, nor need we think we are failing if we are feeling sorrow, numbness, anger, shame and fear. But, there is a point when these feelings become a habitual bias of focusing on the negative, and it feels right to shift this with neural exercises.

Addressing trauma and neglect means we may not be able to hold onto positive experiences for a full 10–20 seconds, as Rick Hanson recommends. Perhaps we can hold onto pleasure for one second, or half of one second, without feeling frozen, disassociating, or being flooded by terror, guilt or shame. We can simply begin wherever we are, and build gradually from that place.

With the *practice* of pleasure, we become more sensitized to pleasure, mentally, physically, emotionally and spiritually. Our whole nervous system is exercised and empowered by expanded pleasure, and we are biophysically and emotionally resourced.

Exercise 75: Body gratitude practice

with thanks to Kristen Myers

Expressing gratitude supports our personal wellbeing. Gratitude practice helps us strengthen connections and build kind and caring communities. If you struggle with body image, a 'body gratitude' practice can help you shift habitual thinking patterns that interfere with your joy.

Breathe in gratitude for your body. Notice the infinitely complicated cooperation of many trillions of differentiated cells that function as a whole within your skin. Feel how your own unique DNA is wound inside the nucleus of every one of these trillions of cells.

Feel your breath; sink into awareness of your breath..... Listen for your heartbeat. Sink into awareness of the blood circulating through your heart and through your whole body.

Notice your food tube; sink into awareness of your digestion..... Relax your jaw, and feel the fluids in your digestive tract. Imagine the peristaltic wave down the tube. Feel the cathedral of your mouth. Feel into your anus.

Notice your belly, and contemplate the many trillions of cells of bacteria in your guts. These creatures have a different DNA and yet are part of you and essential to your living. Contemplate the magnitude of all the unfathomably intricate processes that are going on inside you, allowing you to breathe and move and play..... Give thanks.

Notice whether you have legs that can miraculously move you from one place to another. Flex the muscles of your toes. If you have a disability that involves mobility, notice the means by which you do have movement, the connection between your body and mobility aids. Notice the intricate system of muscles that coordinate when you lift your hand onto your face and caress your eyebrows. Notice the texture of your hair. Feel the inside of your nose. Give thanks.

Notice the skin you are in. Different kinds of nerve cells in the skin respond to different kinds of touch. Notice how you feel light touch..... deeper caress.... go deeper .... try a scratch..... tapping.... a vibration..... Give thanks.

Notice your genitals. Place a hand on them if you can. Feel them from the outside. Try light touch..... deeper caresses....tapping.... vibration..... Give thanks for any sensation.

Breathe into the miracle of having a body.

Exercise 76: Joy jar

with thanks to Sher Snow

Use the drawing on the next page and write inside the jar, or use a real jar and cut up small pieces of paper. Write down 20 things that bring you joy. If you can, make them erotic. Does featherlight touch make you happy? A hot bath? A favorite vibrator? Sexy underwear? An erotic massage? A walk in the forest? A type of porn? A type of poetry? Write down your joys and put them in a jar. Whenever you feel yourself languishing in the habit of negative thoughts or feel distressed by a thorny problem, you can discipline yourself to pick something from your joy jar and do it. If you can't do it right away, you can light up your nervous system by imagining doing it, or making plans to do it.

Variation: Make a 'joy jar' with a partner.

Mix up the papers so you don't know if you will be following one person's joy or another's. Remember to say No to your partner's requests if you need to. Remember you can say Yes and go slowly. You can change your mind at any moment.

Exercise 77: House of memories

Build an imaginary house with different rooms, and dedicate each room to a memory of a time and place you felt happiness in your body. Kindly release any negative judgments about the relationships, or absence of relationships, the simplicity or extravagance of your house. Imagine yourself going into each room and going deeply into a particular pleasurable memory. Savor the textures, tastes, smells, colors... letting each particular memory fill and envelop you.

Exercise 78: Either/or game

with thanks to Marnie Baxter

Get silly and enjoy rapidfire either-or questions and answers. Don't think it over, just spontaneously generate a long list of questions. Enjoy choosing, one after another, as a way to develop trust in your inner guidance system. Notice you do have preferences, and that you can change your mind at any moment.

Sun or moon?
Tangerine or apple?
Bicycle or rowboat?
Green or red?
Pen or bicycle?
Verb or noun?
Clitoris or vagina?
Cock or penis?
River or ocean?

Exercise 79: Sensual preferences

with thanks to Marcia Baczynski

Learn to follow your sensual pleasures with considering only your own self as the reference point (instead of trying to choose what you think might please a partner). What choices offer more pleasure to your senses? Consider sight, sound, smell, taste, touch. What is your favorite color? Your favorite landscape? What are your favorite songs? Practice discerning smells in your environment. Savour the cooking smells you enjoy best. Find three flowers and choose the scent you prefer. Buy three different kinds of apples and do a taste comparison, noticing the difference in textures and flavors. Taste your own sweat on different days, noticing any taste changes with what you eat or drink, or with changes in your anxiety level. Are there ways you taste that you like better? Try tasting your semen or vaginal fluid. Practice touching various objects and textures with your eyes closed, focusing on the exquisite sensations you are feeling. Wear a new or an old sweater just because of how good it feels on your skin.

Exercise 80: Pleasure journal

Every night, write about five things that gave you pleasure during the day.

Exercise 81: Pleasure mandala

Use the image on the following page to make a mandala about your pleasures. Incorporate words, colors and doodled images. Try not to judge your pleasures, just practice noticing and focusing on whatever brings you joy.

Exercise 82: Sexual preferences

Know your sexual preferences are fluid and evolving and can change at any time! Use this page to write about sexual practices you prefer, practices you are curious about and might try in the right circumstances, and sexual things that you have heard about but would never do.

Variation: Do this with a partner or friend, and share your preferences with each other.

Yes	Maybe	Never

EXERCISES FOR EMPOWERING CELLULAR CONSENT

Exercises 83–85 and the concepts in this chapter are drawn from the teachings of Betty Martin. See her website for many more ideas and resources.

Exercise 83: Welcoming the No

It can be hard to find our authentic Yes and follow our pleasure. It can be even harder to negotiate an exchange of pleasures with another person. Asking for what we want puts us in the vulnerable position of possibly hearing No, or being shamed for our desires. We may fear that our request will put someone into a position where they feel they 'should' conform to our wishes. Being able to track our pleasure and then communicate what we want in a highly-charged erotic situation is impossible without practice. This exercise offers an opportunity to practice asking in a fun and irreverent way. Notice what is hard about asking for what you want, and practice so it gets easier and easier.

In this exercise, you will never actually touch. This is practice asking for touch. Ask for any action involving your body and their body. Some examples: May I rub my nose on the bottom of your foot? Would you like me to run my fingers through your hair? Would you like a hug? Can I hug you? Can I jump on your back and ride you around the room like a pony? Get silly. You will always hear No. When you hear No you will always say 'Thank you for taking care of yourself.' Thank them for staying in full heart and communicating what is right for them, and not just mindlessly acquiescing to your request.

A: (Ask for what you want.)

B: No.

A: Thank you for taking care of yourself.

Practice for three minutes, then change roles for another three minutes.

Congratulations! With this exercise you have already done the two hardest things that happen in any rich erotic life—you have asked for what you want, and you have heard No—many times.

Exercise 84: Ask for what you want

Now try something really radical. Practice asking for something that you really do want to do involving touch and this person's body. It might involve a handshake or a very intimate kind of touch. As the one who receives the request, don't answer right away. Take a sacred pause and feel into your pleasure. Is this something you can offer from a place of full heart? You will not actually touch in this exercise, but you will practice making a request and answering a request from a place of full heart. Whatever you hear in response to your request, say thank you.

A: (Take a sacred pause and feel into your heart. Ask for what you want.)

B: (Take a sacred pause and feel into your heart. Answer Yes, No or Maybe.)

A: Thank you.

Notice what is going on inside when you voice a desire. Many of us have a fear of asking, and feel a reluctance to ask. There is a fear of hearing No, and feeling rejected and shamed. Many people second-guess what it is okay to ask for, hoping to keep their offer modest enough so they don't have to hear a No. Or you may be held back by a fear that your ask will be received as a demand, and that the person hearing your request will comply even though they don't want to.

Notice what happens when you respond to someone's voicing of a desire. The desire to serve someone may come up automatically when you hear a request (remember the autonomic nervous system reaction of appease). A sense of refusal/ resistance may come up automatically when you hear someone make a request (remember fight/ flight). Is it different to take the sacred pause, and choose mindfully from a place of full heart, knowing you can change your mind at any moment?

STAYING IN FULL HEART

To create an environment where we can ask freely, we need to make a basic agreement that neither partner will go into enduring mode. Enduring is a 'default' mode for sexual experience in our culture. People learn to endure because of:

- People's discomfort with sex and their own desires
- Power dynamics
- The social and emotional needs we bring to sexual relationships
- The widespread incidence of sexual violence, chronic trauma, oppression and neglect

We may never have had a chance to explore and discover what we prefer and what Yes and No feel like.

Whether you are touching or being touched, stay in full heart with what you are offering. Know that you can change your mind at any moment, and do that, even if it's hard sometimes, because if you don't you won't be staying in full heart. Make an agreement with yourself that that you will honor your feelings as they unfold from moment-to-moment, and remain in alignment with yourself by communicating them. Make an agreement with your partner that they won't 'yuck your yum,' and judge or shame you for what you want, even if it's something they need to say No to. We can ask more easily when the consequences of revealing our desires are limited. We can find and say a heartfelt Yes more easily when we understand there is no expectation or compulsion to say Yes. We can say No more easily when we know that our refusal will be met with gratitude. By thanking people for their No as well as their Yes, we help to create an environment where people can really learn to follow their pleasure, experiment and explore, and stay in a place of full heart.

What empowers us to follow the inner Yes and trust the inner No?

- Slowing down—attending to the inner world
- Clarity of communication
- Safety—agreement not to shame, agreement to stay in full heart with our gifts
- Confidence in our ability to make a change
- Practice, practice, practice

What keeps us out of the moment-to-moment process of being in full heart with ourselves?

- Managing expectations
- Low self-esteem
- Lack of confidence
- Power imbalance

Keep catching yourself when you slip into following your usual scripts for touch. Keep affirming your openness to change. Celebrate your own No's and your partner's No's. Welcome any change of mind.

Exercise 85: How would you like to be touched?

Take ten minutes and work with a partner. Agree that they will touch you, but only in ways that you guide them. They won't touch you in any way that you have not guided them. They will do their best to follow your directions and touch you in whatever way you ask for, within their boundaries, while staying in full heart with their touch.

Lie down with eyes closed and have them ask you, 'How would you like to be touched?' Sink into the question and feel the answer from the inside. Notice that your body does have information for you, if you listen. Wait patiently until you get a sense of how you would like to be touched, and then see if you can use your words to guide them. Notice if it is hard to guide them, if you feel listened to, if you start worrying about their comfort and pleasure.

Have them keep asking, 'How would you like to be touched?' Working with this question can be a powerful learning experience. With patient practice, we can put an end to enduring, and feel and speak our truth in erotic exchanges.

Variation: Do by yourself.

Variation: Try a shorter or longer session. Set a timer for three minutes, ten minutes and thirty minutes.

Exercise 86: Pleasure mapping

Pleasure mapping is another exercise that can help us to experience arousal mindfully while communicating with another. Mapping begins with one partner—the 'pleasure receiver'—resting on a bed or a massage table. The other partner is the 'pleasure researcher.' The researcher touches a series of places on the receiver's body. In response to each touch, the receiver communicates—by a number of fingers extended on the right or left hand—the degree of desirability or undesirability of each sensation. You can also use vocal expression (plus three, minus three, neutral, etc.). The experience of tuning in and paying attention to what truly feels pleasurable is as important as the opportunity to courageously communicate the nuances of pleasure.

EVOLVING THE NERVOUS SYSTEM WITH TOUCH

Animal and human studies prove again and again that lots of touch is essential for self-regulation, autonomic stability and psychosocial wellbeing. Both touch deprivation and touch trauma affect brain tissue development in a way that neurologically primes us for future trauma. Neuroplasticity, however, means that we can work and play to change our brains and nervous systems throughout life. Studies show that frequent pleasurable touch is associated with enhanced learning, immune system health, language acquisition, social skills acquisition, cardiac health and many other benefits.

People who respond to trauma and neglect with a nervous system stuck on 'high' can experience even very gentle touch as stressful and retraumatizing. People whose nervous system has adapted to trauma and neglect by shutting down and getting stuck on 'low' may need strong touch and bold sensation to feel pleasure. If we can find a way—any way—to enjoy touch, then we can follow our pleasure, and gradually expand our pleasure with diverse sensation, as our nervous system grows and evolves in response to pleasurable touch.

Nerves that go numb in response to trauma or neglect can come alive with pleasurable stimulation. Nerves that have become hypersensitive in response to trauma and neglect can gradually learn to accept touch joyfully. By following our pleasure with self-touch, or with a partner who is responsive to verbal and non-verbal directions, we are helping our nervous system evolve and become capable of feeling more.

Learning New Attachment Patterns

Our capacity for healthy loving relationships is profoundly affected by trauma, oppression and neglect. Our experiences in relationships shape our physiology, alter the functioning of our autonomic nervous system, and even have an impact on our genes.

LOVE IS FOUNDATIONAL

"Love is clearly not 'just' an emotion," note scientists Sue Carter and Stephen Porges. Love is a biological process. "[T]he body seeks love and responds constantly to interaction with loved ones or to the absence of such interaction."

Love is crucial to our survival. As newborn humans we are completely dependent on our caregivers. We are vulnerable and dependent much longer than most mammals. The care of others is what creates enough safety for our bodies, brains and nervous systems to evolve into somewhat independent, self-regulating systems.

The 'fear detector' in the brain, the amygdala, is fully developed before we are born. In utero we feel autonomic nervous system cycles of peace and excitement, fear and pleasure. But the cortical structures that allow us to interpret and regulate body sensations and reactions don't develop until many years later. (The cerebral cortex adds 70 per cent of its mass after birth and grows to 90 per cent of its adult size during our first three years of life.) When feeling fear and deep distress, an infant cannot 'know' how to comfort itself. Threats activate sympathetic nervous system hyperarousal, increasing heart rate, blood pressure, and respiration. This hyperarousal can be soothed when a caregiver's loving attention and pleasant touch generates an inner bath of love hormones to calm the inner bath of stress hormones. Oxytocin in particular lowers autonomic distress.

When reassuring reconnection with a loving caregiver reliably follows short periods of distress, an infant eventually learns to calm its own distressed nervous system, self-reassure and self-regulate. We biophysically learn that separation does not mean ongoing distress but only a period of challenge that will be followed by more comfort and connection. Thus we literally build our individual nervous systems with the help of loving relationship. Secure attachment, together with manageable challenge, build biophysical systems that offer an internal locus of control.

Ongoing interdependence

Our nervous systems are never completely independent. Throughout life, we remain neurologically linked with other people and with the environment. Our physical and emotional well-being is profoundly shaped by the proximity of a tree, a pet or a friend. Our nervous systems are always regulated by participation in social groups. There are biophysical mechanisms through which this happens.

'Mirror neurons' light up in our brains as if we were feeling pain when we see another's injury, and the same is true for joy. There is real neurological pleasure in others' pleasure; our brains light up as if we are actually experiencing sexual pleasure and orgasm when we watch someone else experience sexual pleasure and orgasm.

Our autonomic nervous systems are continually responding to each other, so that we become calmer by being in calm connection with another person, and more bold in a courageous group. We are affected by how the people around us breathe, eat, play, express themselves sexually, and whether they feel happiness or loneliness. So it makes sense that we build nervous system capacity to feel deeply and regulate our autonomic states through social relationships with others.

Relationships help us build flexibility and resilience when they support excitement, novelty and adventure while providing a path back to safety. When social relationships are unstable or unsafe, our nervous systems will be less resilient and self-regulating.

ATTACHMENT PATTERNS

The quality and quantity of love available in early relationships shapes our biophysical response to others: our vigilance, our fear, our habitual tendency to feel playful, distressed, alienated or cherished. Children develop attachment styles, which can be described as either 'secure' or 'insecure.' A child with a secure attachment style feels consistently connected with loving caregivers. They have a sense of their own independence as well as trust and attunement with their tribe. Children who are not so fortunate usually develop insecure attachment styles that can be further differentiated as avoidant, anxious and disorganized. Attachment styles established in childhood can set habitual relationship patterns throughout life. These attachment styles are not grooved in stone but rather in the living cells and electrical and chemical signals of each person's nervous system, and so they are plastic and can be changed. Often people recognize parts of themselves in all the attachment styles. We can have different perspectives and attachment habits with different people.

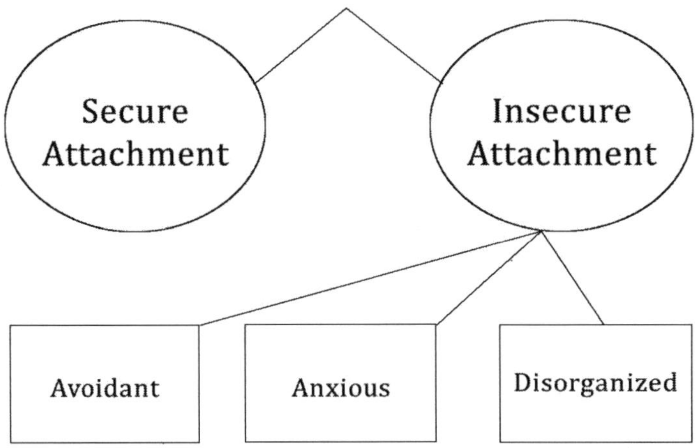

Figure 14: Attachment styles

Secure attachment

When you are coming from the perspective of secure attachment, it is much easier for you to regulate your emotions and be the person you want to be. You are relaxed with being alone, and you really enjoy your relationships. You care deeply and passionately, without feeling stuck in fighting for what you want and believe in. Sexually, you are playful, and not unduly constrained by social sanctions. You can ask for what you want from a partner. You are likely to do what's necessary to practice safer sex, and to protect yourself from unwanted pregnancies. You enjoy experimenting with different erotic scripts and expanding your repertoire by learning new things. You are a consistent and reliable relationship partner who is also curious and fun. You understand that other people can't always come from this secure perspective, and that they sometimes need forgiveness and loving support. When things don't work out in relationships, you can still feel gratitude for all that the partnerships have given you.

Avoidant attachment

When you are coming from the perspective of avoidant attachment, you will tend to be the center of your own universe: self-absorbed and relatively dismissive of the importance of love and relationship. You live in your head and suppress your feelings. Your relationship partners might get angry, jealous, and want more from you. You will tend to feel repelled rather than compelled by their arguments, and distance yourself from them emotionally. Sexually you will be happiest with undemanding relationships. You might be comfortable with long-term casual sex or a secret affair. You will have trouble saying Yes to opportunities for profound connection. As for sexual scripts, you will soar most easily when exploring erotic trance and sinking deeply into your own self-awareness. (See 'Dimensions of sexual experience' in the chapter 'Sex Outside the Box.') Practices like erotic massage and mindful self-pleasuring feel like home. It's hard for you to communicate your desires and ask for change from a sexual partner. When you feel needy or hurt, you want to isolate. When things don't work out, you feel it was probably inevitable, and grateful it doesn't matter that much to you.

There are gifts in this perspective. You have great independence and lots of emotional insulation to keep you feeling safe and self-sufficient when things aren't joyful. But you can challenge yourself to reach outside of your bubble and try on different perspectives. You might try getting more curious about others. See if you can use some of the exercises in this book to feel more grounded and safe when someone offers you a hug or bares their soul to you. Notice if your partner's sexual needs are different from yours. Try gently engaging with sexual scripts that are more challenging for you, cultivating some capacity in partner engagement and role play.

Anxious attachment

When you are coming from the perspective of anxious attachment you will tend to be *preoccupied* with your relationships. Other people always seem to love you inadequately. Their reassurance never really relieves your doubt and self-doubt. You are worried, jealous and untrusting. You want to cling. If things aren't working out, you can feel desperate, shaken to the core. Sexually, you soar when you are the center of someone's world. Partner engagement practices touch you deeply. You love serving others. You will have trouble saying No. You talk things over (and sometimes over and over), but communicating your authentic needs is difficult because you are so afraid of rejection.

There are gifts in this perspective. Because relationships are so important to you, you might be the one who convenes family gatherings, or keeps a marriage together. You are likely to be a loyal long-term partner, though relationships without passion and intensity don't work that well for you.

When you feel a familiar need for reassurance from others, you can challenge yourself to focus instead on your own internal sense of safety. Feel your inner self-support. Use the practices from the chapter on 'Creating Safe Zones' to feel more at home and resourced in your own skin. Sexually, try occasionally letting go of your focus on partner connection, and tuning into your own body experience. Erotic massage and mindful self-pleasuring will help you feel more erotically independent and in touch with your own sensations. If masturbation leaves you cold, you can try masturbating alongside a friend. Forays into role-play might help you try on new perspectives. Watch for any tendency to feel hurt and demeaned by role-play scenarios. Try saying No. Try on some rose-colored glasses and really pay attention to all the small and large ways you are cared for in your relationships and communities. You might not be getting exactly what you want, but all the love you receive *can* support and nourish you, if you let it.

Disorganized attachment

A child might develop a disorganized attachment pattern if they have violent and abusive caretakers, or if they can't find a strategy that works with unpredictable caregivers. From the perspective of disorganized attachment, relationships are often chaotic. You might get angry easily, startle easily, yell or snap at people, feel you don't belong anywhere, be despairing, moody, fearful, or be frightening to others. Sometimes you feel immobilized, disconnected, or 'gone.' You crave intimacy and you fear it. You vacillate between saying Yes and No—never quite sure what is right for you. It's easy for you to ignore your own instincts. Instead of defending yourself or getting away from situations that could be dangerous for you, you are liable to dissociate and get confused. Instead of moving towards the love and pleasure that is possible in your present circumstances, you are liable to pick a fight or focus on what isn't working. Sexually, it is hard to follow your pleasure or even notice your pleasure when you masturbate. Being sexual with others is even more challenging.

When your 'disorganized attachment' perspective gets activated, you will likely need therapeutic help and support. You can also use the exercises in this book to help calm the inner chaos of chronic autonomic nervous system hyperarousal and change habits of reactivity and dissociation.

LEARNING NEW ATTACHMENT PATTERNS

Whatever your habit or attachment perspective in a given relationship or situation, you can learn to invoke other perspectives. Use your 'compassionate witness' consciousness, so that you can take your emotions seriously without getting derailed by them. Welcome awareness of your anxieties and attachment patterns, and sit 'holding' your feelings as if you are holding a frightened animal. Let your frightened animal self become calm enough to look around and know whether it is or isn't necessary, in this moment, to fight, flee, appease, freeze or dissociate. Notice that your insecure attachment patterns get activated when your need to belong and gain the loving support of your fellow humans is conflicting with your drive to survive as an independent being. From a calmer and more detached place, the seat of compassionate witness, you gain more choice in how you will act to meet your basic needs for safety, belonging and dignity.

Trauma and attachment therapist Diane Poole Heller urges us to see that a capacity for secure attachment is already present in each one of us. This capacity can be cultivated, even though there are wounds in the way. "We see that Secure Attachment is there already.... We can excavate it and support it and learn how to be with ourselves and others from this natural secure space more and more." From the secure attachment perspective "it's easy to be playful, we can share our love and connection, there's an easy flow into relationship and an easy flow into autonomy. We don't feel stressed when people approach us or stressed when people separate from us.... We have an unflappability about us when we're in our Secure Attachment." From the perspective of secure attachment, we have more comfort with ourselves and more attunement with—or compassion for—others. Although early life experiences make deep grooves in our nervous systems and shape our habits in relationships, simply by knowing and recognizing the attachment perspectives we are embodying, we can learn to better give and receive love, cultivate joy, and foster our sense of secure attachment.

We will love you until you learn to love yourself

Research on adverse childhood experiences directly links the early experience of abuse and neglect with a predisposition to mental and physical illnesses of all kinds, and impaired functioning over a lifespan. Good-enough early relationships definitely give us a head start. Without the internal bath of neurochemicals that carry a biological message of 'love' throughout the body and brain of a well-loved infant, we don't develop strong internal self-regulating mechanisms. Our lives and relationships, our sexuality and pleasure, all are profoundly shaped by our anxieties. Sue Carter and Stephen Porges note that "Love is an epigenetic phenomenon: social behaviors, emotional attachment to others and long-lasting reciprocal relationships are plastic and adaptive and so is the biology on which they are based...." Chronic exposure to stress-related neurochemicals in infancy can create a life-long tendency to overreact to threat. If you experienced trauma, oppression and neglect as an infant, you will likely have an increased sensitivity to stress and anxiety that will persist throughout life.

But the good news is that every relationship—with a friend, a lover, a therapist, a service provider, a workshop, a community—offers a chance to rewire relational habits and bathe ourselves in the biological message of love. If we can recognize and gently release the insecure attachment patterns that prevent us from really feeling the love of others, we can foster our allegiance to secure attachment, and gain familiarity with the internal states that help us perceive love and give and receive love.

In recovery communities there is a saying that 'We will love you until you learn to love yourself.' Twelve-step groups make a commitment to love each member just as they are, including all the dysfunctions and mistakes. In an environment of unconditional acceptance, shame loses its grip and self-hatred cannot flourish. Empowered by the group's love, people can learn to use the tools of recovery programs to change habits they embody, and become the people they want to be.

Are there relationships or communities where you feel loved and cherished? Do you have a dog, a therapist, a special friend? Try really absorbing any experiences of being loved that you can find and create. Drink them into your body and soul. In any relationship, we can focus on ways our experience of love is provisional, temporary, or partial (i.e. we can see things from the perspective of insecure attachment). What if we make a commitment instead to focus on how the experience of love is beautiful, soothing, healing and profound (i.e. stand in the perspective of secure attachment)? In this process, we teach our nervous system how it feels to be secure and to belong. We can build a basic sense of inner 'okayness' that we were not able to access in a childhood marked by trauma and neglect.

Love does not have to be perfect or permanent in order to heal and transform us. Just as an infant builds an autonomous capacity for self-regulation through soothing experiences of connection and loving touch with imperfect caregivers, so can we as adults. We only require temporary and 'good-enough' experiences of love and belonging to begin building an internal locus of control. With expanded capacity for self-regulation, we can create more choice in our attachment patterns, and establish new neural grooves for soothing our anxieties, so that we feel ourselves flourishing in solitude and in relationships, and experience more pleasure, contentment and joy.

Exercise 87: Constellation of love and belonging

See if you can create an image about how you love and are loved, and how you belong, using the stars on the following page.

See if there are places of belonging that you have within and around you, perhaps with companion animals, favorite writers, or in relationships with people where you are partially seen and imperfectly loved. Do you feel a sense of love and belonging in the natural world? Are there cultures, communities, circles of influence, circles of concern that you live inside and are part of? Notice how you feel untrusting, and how you feel relaxed in your body, when considering different people, environments and commitments.

Use colors, words and doodles around the stars. At first it can feel hard and overwhelming to contemplate, if you have been focused on how you are unloved and don't belong. Take your time and document what is there for you.

Safety plus Manageable Challenge

"Being able to feel safe with other people is probably the single most important aspect of mental health; safe connections are fundamental to meaningful and satisfying lives," psychiatrist Bessel van der Kolk explains. Without a sense of safety, we stay physiologically dysregulated. "For our physiology to calm down, heal and grow we need a visceral feeling of safety." Safety is essential if we are to learn and change neural patterns established in infancy. But, safety in itself is not enough for learning to take place. Challenge is also essential. If we stay stuck in habitual grooves where we *only* feel safe, we experience nervous system atrophy. If we are never challenged to learn self-soothing, we never have a chance to develop the biochemical responses and cortical structures that allow for self-regulation. If we always face unmanageable challenges, we can only learn to collapse and dissociate. That is why it is so important that the challenges we tackle are manageable within our personal, particular learning zone, where we are often uncomfortable, but not unsafe.

Exercise 88: Seeing the good in others

Write down the names of ten people in your life along with one thing you like or admire about each person. Share it with that person in a card or in a conversation. Seeing the goodness and beauty in others is a basic element of creating an inner allegiance to secure attachment patterns. Sharing the goodness and beauty you see is good for you and good for them.

ATTACHMENT AND SEX

Safety, belonging and dignity are fundamental and constitutive human needs, deeply embedded in the nervous system, driving all human interactions. People often feel conflicted about how to meet these fundamental needs when it comes to sex and sexual identity. Do you hide your passions or stay small (and lose dignity) in order to belong? Do you eschew belonging and stay isolated in order to feel safe? Do you claim the dignity of being who you really feel yourself to be, erotically, at the expense of safety and belonging?

We learn by synchronizing emotionally and physically with others. When we are isolated by our sexual identity, experience or desires, and don't see ourselves mirrored and taken into account by our communities, we can internalize a sense of not belonging anywhere.

So few of us have loving and competent caregivers and communities that support our flourishing in the realm of sex and sexuality. When we have not had the opportunity to be affirmed and cherished in our own unique sexual identity, our capacity for sexual connection with others is impaired. Fear of sexual intimacy and patterns of clinging to sexual partners or closing our hearts to deep feeling (anxious or avoidant attachment patterns) get wired into our nervous systems.

Neural patterns cannot be changed by cognitive insights into how they were created. We can understand that our fearfulness, detachment or desperation in sexual relationships is rooted in trauma or neglect, but actually opening up to others in healthy ways may stay inaccessible without the actual, embodied experience of loving erotic connection. Embodied experiences of attunement with others are what allow our physiology to heal and change. With a willingness to make mistakes, and trying to stay within our learning zone, we can slowly begin to notice and reveal who we are sexually. We can gradually find our tribe and build connections with others who are available for safe, exploratory erotic connection.

Exercise 89: Get noticed

Not being seen can be damaging to our wellbeing and self-esteem. But being seen and noticed can feel very risky. Try doing something that gets your erotic identity noticed. Remember to play within your learning zone.

Some possibilities:

- Color your hair purple
- Wear a low-cut dress
- Wear a badge
- Go to a sex toy store
- Phone somebody and talk about sex
- Wink at someone
- Tell someone how sexy they are

Pick the right level of risk for you. Pay attention to your body sensation. Afterwards, reflect on how it felt in your body to get noticed.

Exercise 90: Sexual orientation

What qualities and characteristics draw your erotic attention? What and who do you orient to? Do you pay attention to signs of sexual and sensual energy exchange between you and other people in your life? Are you always oriented to signs of potential danger? Do you pay attention to moments and manifestations of beauty in other people, relationships and the environment? Spend time over several days just noticing and documenting what you orient towards. Notice what happens in your body when you orient to different cues. Decide if you want to adjust your orientation.

What and who do you orient to that helps you feel good and safe? How does that feel in your body?

What and who do you orient to that gets your erotic juices flowing? How does that feel in your body?

What and who do you orient to that feels scary and unsafe? How does that feel in your body?

What and who do you orient to that stops your erotic juices from flowing? How does that feel in your body?

What and who do you *want* to pay more attention to? How might this adjustment in your orientation affect your body?

Exercise 91: Write a new story

In an earlier chapter you were invited to share your sexual story with a non-judgmental person (or animal or place). Now try writing and sharing a new story, one that focuses on your experience as a hero's journey. You have been separated from the ordinary world by a terrible trial. You have faced extraordinary dangers. What gifts have you returned with? Has your experience deepened your compassion, or shaped your commitments? How has it enhanced your capacity for joy? Think of the difficult material of your life as compost. What extraordinary aspects of you have been fed by this nourishing (if slimy) stuff?

BODY LANGUAGE

To get playful in relationships and learn new attachment styles, we need to become good communicators. These exercises are offered as yet another way to follow our inner Yes and to trust our inner No and then to share that with others. Only a small percentage of our communication is in words. Facial expressions, vocal tones, posture and gesture communicate so much, but people recovering from trauma and neglect may have a decreased ability to read nonverbal cues and to communicate their feelings in body language.

Exercise 92: Say No with your body

Pat Ogden and Janina Fisher offer a list of ways we say No and set a boundary with our bodies. I have modified their list slightly.

Shake head	Furrow brow, frown, scowl	Lean back, move away	Tone of voice
Purse lips	Clench jaw	Look down or away	Aggressive posture
Laugh, snicker	Push, hit	Narrow, roll or close eyes	Square shoulders or hunch forward
Tighten body	Stern facial expression	Turn away	Snort
Move head back	Sigh with exasperation	Raise eyebrows	Wrinkle nose (disgust)
Chin forward	Hands make a 'Stop' gesture	Hands clench	Tailbone tucked in, cross legs or pull legs together
Cover ears	Make 'X' with forefingers	Thumbs down	Waving a forefinger back and forth

Study the list and then play with saying No with your body. Are there ways you say No that aren't on the list? Add them. Saying No is important when we need to defend ourselves against real threats and set boundaries in our relationships. Saying No can also be an embodied habit, a 'fight or flight' response that prevents us from connecting deeply with others and with life.

Write down memories you have of times you felt No and said No with your body, but your No wasn't seen or 'heard' by a sexual partner. Notice how you say No with your body in different situations in your everyday life, without actually speaking your No. Are there situations in your everyday life where your No is not getting understood by others? What about by you—are you listening when your body says No? Does your body say No more than your voice? Do you say No more or less than you really want to? How does this relate to your erotic life?

Exercise 93: Saying Yes with your body

Pat Ogden and Janina Fisher offer a list of ways we can say Yes and make an invitation to others with our bodies. I have modified their list slightly.

Nod head	Raise brows	Smile	Smiling eyes, widened eyes
Tilt head to one side (expose jugular)	Make eye contact	Arms open (expose heart)	Reach out
Move towards	Turn towards	Soften muscles of the face	Blink eyes
Deep breath with a long exhale	Hands up (can mean 'Hello' or 'I surrender')	Thumbs up	Hands open or extended
Beckoning gesture	Wag tailbone, shake hips	Settle in seated postion	Spread legs wide

Study the list and then play with saying Yes with your body. Are there ways you say Yes that aren't on the list? Add them. Saying Yes is important when we want to welcome pleasure into our lives and connect deeply with others. However, saying Yes can also be a habit of appeasement that prevents us from defending ourselves against real threats and setting appropriate boundaries in our relationships.

Write down any memories you have of times you said Yes as a way of appeasing a sexual partner, and afterwards you wished you had said No. Are there any times you felt Yes in an embodied and heartfelt way, wanting to welcome deeper connection and intimacy, but your silent Yes wasn't seen or 'heard'? Notice how you say Yes with your body in different situations in your everyday life, without actually speaking your Yes. Are there situations in your everyday life where your Yes is not getting understood by others? Does your body say Yes more or less than your voice? Do you say Yes more or less that you really want to? How does this relate to your erotic life?

PARTNER EXERCISES

Exercise 94: Intuiting the energetic boundary with another person

Stand on opposite sides of the room. Feel your rootedness. Intuit your energetic boundary. Look at your partner. Keep tracking your boundary—how does looking at the other person affect your felt sense of this boundary? If it feels safe enough, beckon them slowly closer to you with your hand. Stop when you want to. Send them back and see how your feelings shift. Feel what it's like to be in charge of whether or not to allow this person to come closer to you.

Variation: Use colored ribbons on the floor to create a boundary around yourself. Say aloud, 'This is my boundary. You may come beyond it only if I invite you in. I can change my mind and get you out at any time.'

Exercise 95: Boundary defense

with thanks to Peter Levine

From the exercise above, find a comfortable place that feels like your boundary with this person. Now play with defending your boundary. Have the person approaching you try to 'get inside' your boundary while you push back. Start slowly. Feel the strength in your center, your rooted feet, as you push back against the boundary incursion by your partner.

Take turns playing the role of boundary defense and boundary incursion person. When you are the boundary incursion person, if you sense that the boundary defender is collapsing or backing off, reduce your push and limit your incursion strategies until you feel the boundary defender has regained strength. If they are strong, get playful and fierce about your boundary incursions. Try different strategies. Try just one toe, try pushing with force, get wily, act sad. See if you can get inside.

Change roles, beginning with the exercise on 'Intuiting the energetic boundary with another person' and proceeding to 'Boundary defense.'

Variation: invite and resist the person with sound.

Exercise 96: Connection

Explore connecting with another person physically. This table takes you through a sequence in which we can really practice noticing how we feel in our bodies as we increase the intensity of our physical connection with another person.

Energy	Posture	Movement	Casual Touch	Intimate Touch
Back to Back	Open posture	Extend arms	Finger touch	Hug
Side to Side	Mirror other's posture	Move closer	Handshake	Cling
Face to Face	Head up, interested expression, eye contact	Reach /lean towards	Shoulder touch	Hold and Pet

Exercise 97: Mirror neurons

Each person stands in their own space, near but not close enough to touch their partner. Partner A leads and Partner B follows, mirroring their movements and facial expressions. Change roles.

Variation: Add sound, exploring and mirroring different tones.

Exercise 98: Circulating breath with a partner

Conscious breathing together can enhance connection, soothe conflicts, and bring vitality and energy into your relationship. Breathing together reflects and enhances the attunement of our autonomic nervous systems. We can co-regulate and help each other to surf waves of calmness and excitement.

This is a good exercise to do with a partner right after brushing your teeth, so you won't be self-conscious about your breath.

Sit opposite each other, your legs intertwined comfortably. Get your faces close. Breathe in through your nose and out through your mouth. Let your jaws relax and get slack. Look at each other's eyes with a soft, unfocused gaze that only sees beauty and goodness. Close your eyes whenever you want to.

As you are breathing in through your nose and out through your mouth, you can make a little sound on the exhale.

As one person breathes out through the mouth, the other person breathes in. Catch their breath, and breathe it into your body.

As one breathes out, one breathes in.

You are circling your breath, creating a circle of energy between you.

If you lose your rhythm, just smile and get it back.

If you want to laugh, smile, touch as you breathe—do it.

Do whatever is fun and joyful.

Stay with the practice long enough to get over your giggles and awkward feelings, but not so long that you feel uncomfortable.

When you're done, take time to hold each other and share a few words about what you enjoyed and what made you feel silly or weird.

'Gotcha!'

with thanks to Staci Haines and the Strozzi Institute

A 'Gotcha!' is a disconcerting challenge, an unexpected problem, or a catch. Throughout the day, every day, there are plenty of 'Gotcha!' moments. How do we tend to respond? With the perception of challenge we might feel a desire to appease and accommodate. We can feel an urge to confront and wrestle with the challenge. We might have a desire to flee, or a sense of collapse and paralysis, a 'going elsewhere' in our minds, going numb. All of these are valid and immensely valuable autonomic nervous system responses, aspects of embodied wisdom, and wonderful resources in various situations. As survivors of trauma and neglect, we tend to get stuck in specific patterns when it comes to responding to erotic 'Gotcha!' moments. Awareness of our embodied habits gives us more choice.

'Gotcha!' is a challenging partner exercise that can bring up strong feelings. People who feel unready for this experience, and those who don't have a partner to practice with, can imagine what would happen if they were to do this exercise and journal about their feelings. For those who choose to engage in a 'Gotcha!' exercise, be sure to create an agreement about what will happen before you do it.

Exercise 99: Eye contact 'Gotcha!'

Person A stands still, grounding and centering themselves in place. Person B approaches them from the front, looking at their body appreciatively, saying their name, and seeking eye contact. For people who have experienced trauma, eye contact is often felt as an aggression. Person A tracks what they feel in their body, feeling whether they are recoiling away from (to flee? to refuse?) or turning to meet (to appease? to connect?) person B, or collapsing within themselves. Track body movements, emotions and sensations.

Exercise 100: Ass-slapping 'Gotcha!'

Person A stands still, grounding and centering themselves in place. Person B approaches them from behind, calls out the name of person A, and at the same time, slaps them on the buttock. Person A tracks how they react within themselves—moving away from or turning towards Person B, or feeling a sense of 'caving in.'

Now Person A reflects on the way

their nervous system responded to the 'Gotcha!' Did you experience fear or anger, surrender or withdrawal? Can you describe your response as fight, flight, appease, freeze or dissociate? Or something else? How did this feel in your body? Reflect on what your observations in this exercise reveal about your habitual responses to others. What gets you? How do you get caught?

The 'Gotcha!' exercise is an inquiry into our neural patterns and embodied habits.

We can offer our embedded autonomic nervous system reactions our deep respect, and also cultivate possibilities for more choice.

Sex Outside the Box

Even if we have painstakingly and playfully transformed our readiness to reconnect with ourselves and others sexually, we are very likely to face a lack of opportunities to explore and express our erotic needs. The existing models for sexual exchange and sexual relationship are often inadequate for people who are reconnecting with sex. We live in a culture where sexual imagery is everywhere, but opportunities for caring sexual connections are infrequent—especially when we are neither young and beautiful, nor rich and powerful. Furthermore, there are only two models for erotic relationships that are widely recognized as possibilities. In one highly-valued model, sex is an expression of romantic love in a monogamous relationship. In another widely-traded model, sex is an expression of appetite in a soul-free 'hookup.' Part of the personal and cultural reconnection with sex involves imagining new forms of sexual relationship and creating new avenues for erotic expression.

The existing models of sexual relationship are inadequate for anyone who experiences a lack of romance, a fear of romance, or a dearth of willing partners. Some people are committed to an existing partnership in which sex is not possible or not pleasurable. Creating a new sexual culture, we can imagine possibilities for caring sexual connections that do not require romantic relationships. We can develop ways to meet and exchange erotic touch without needing to be found attractive and get 'chosen' for sex. People are also inhibited by a fear of inadequacy. By challenging the intercourse imperative and other performance-oriented models of sexual interaction, we open up a bigger field of possibility for pleasure and address multiple performance anxieties. We can create new sexual culture that values diverse people, ages, body types and abilities.

Even without trauma memories, most people are inhibited by a fear of bad sex, emerging from way too many experiences of enduring uncomfortable, uneducated touch. New paradigms for sexual interaction can help us put an end to enduring. We can explore erotic pleasures in ways that empower our choice and voice. We can also understand that good sex comes as a consequence of learning to have good sex, both in general terms, and in an ongoing unfolding with each partner. We have a strange belief that sex should be instinctive. Good sex comes from study and practice.

SEXUAL PRACTICES OUTSIDE THE BOX

PVI

People tend to equate the word 'sex' with 'partner sex.' Furthermore, heterosexually-identified people often imagine that 'sex' is equivalent with 'penis-in-vagina intercourse' (PVI). People often come to see me complaining that they 'can't have sex' when issues like erectile dysfunction or pelvic pain prevent them from engaging in PVI. A quick fix can be had by reconceptualizing sex so that it involves hands, mouths, toys and self-pleasure. Often, the problem is not so simple. Complaints of 'sexual dysfunction' frequently screen a history of abuse and neglect: people are shut down and turned off erotically because of the trauma their body holds and the autonomic nervous system dysregulation they embody.

PVI is a high-pressure practice that requires both participants to be highly turned-on and relaxed at the same time. It can be a difficult practice for survivors to navigate joyfully. There needs to be a high level of sympathetic nervous system arousal (excitement) to generate focus and intensity. Simultaneously, there needs to be sufficient parasympathetic nervous system arousal (contentment) so that autonomic nerves in the genitals can relax the blood vessels, allowing for engorgement and erection of genital tissues. As we have explored in previous chapters, as survivors of trauma and neglect we often need practice expanding our experience of excitement without slipping over the edge into anxiety, and expanding our experience of contentment without zoning out and dissociating. Most survivors—and indeed most people who grow up in our culture—have little practice using their voice to ask for what they want and need in the midst of *any* sexual exchange. Tracking our pleasure and communicating our choices in the midst of highly charged sexual exchanges like PVI can feel impossible.

PVI tends to be hurried by both partners' worries over whether the penetrating partner can get and sustain an erection for a long enough time to enable intromission and copulation. All too often this results in a hurried encounter in which the receptive partner's arousal anatomy is insufficiently stimulated and inadequately lubricated. Many men have habituated themselves to require a lot of friction to maintain erection and to orgasm. Obtaining this kind of high-intensity friction through consensual PVI can feel uncomfortable and even violent for the receptive partner. Vaginal injuries are common in voluntary sex, and they can cause scarring, desensitization and chronic pain. Painful consensual sex can trigger trauma memories and retraumatize survivors.

Challenging the intercourse imperative opens up a bigger field of possibility for pleasure. It addresses multiple performance anxieties, as well as anxieties about pregnancy and sexually transmitted infections. The vast majority of women (80 per cent) do not climax through PVI alone.

Sexual practices outside the box of PVI are often easier to navigate for survivors of trauma and neglect. Autonomous sex, slower and more sensuous partner practices, and highly communicative interactions can be a better fit for people whose autonomic nervous system is prone to dysregulation.

Whether we personally enjoy it or not, PVI is simply not the ultimate sex act, and people can enjoy full and free sexual lives without ever engaging in PVI.

Autonomous sex

Ultrasound imaging shows that fetuses in utero masturbate to orgasm. Infants and children enjoy genital self-pleasuring unless shamed and forbidden by socio-cultural forces. Self-pleasuring is a key part of nervous system development from the time touch-sensing neurons form in fetal development (as early as 7 weeks) through adulthood until death. But masturbation has been held in low regard through the history of Western culture. In the theological model, masturbation was a sin. In the medical model, masturbation was said to cause disease. The fight against masturbation reached an apex of violence in the late 19th century. Brutalities like clitoridectomy, penis piercing, and spiked penis sheaths were employed to prevent and punish masturbation.

Circumcision of infant boys was one of the practices promoted to stamp out masturbation through medical violence.

Shockingly, this brutality continues today, despite new scientific understanding of the vulnerability of the infant brain and nervous system, and the lifelong consequences of early-life trauma. In North America between 50 and 60 per cent of newborn male infants are circumcised, violently excising the most sensitive parts of the penis.

Alongside this commonplace act of violent trauma, there is a culture of profound neglect. Children's early experiences with masturbation are all too often met with alarm or disapproval from parents.

Psycho-social stigmatizing of masturbation as immature and second-best continues to be commonplace. Religious, medical and psychological filters continue to inhibit people's experiences with self-sexuality. This shows up in unreasonably low levels of adults enjoying self-pleasuring practices. A recent study based on a representative sample of American adults found only 38 per cent of women said they'd masturbated at all during the past year. The figure for men was 61 per cent. And of those who do masturbate, how many truly savour and enjoy the experience fully?

Exercise 101: Self-pleasure practice

Developing an autonomous sexual practice is an important key to reclaiming erotic pleasure. I encourage clients to make love to themselves, gently seducing and passionately coaxing themselves to come alive erotically. Self-pleasuring can happen quickly or extend through hours-long elaborate rituals. We can explore whole body touch, erotic breath, erotic visualization, and stimulating the genitals with a wide variety of techniques I have described in my book *Erotic Massage* and online courses. Or we can stimulate ourselves in habitual and reliable ways. For reconnecting with sex in the wake of trauma and neglect, what matters is not any particular technique for self-pleasure, but that we *practice* self-pleasure, understanding that all forms of masturbation are normal, ethical, responsible, healing and potentially joyful.

One client, a trauma survivor, could not use her hands to pleasure herself without triggering trauma memories and going numb. But she enjoyed romancing herself, and found she could come alive with pleasure when she bought herself flowers and treated herself to dinner. We do not need to judge and compare our pleasures, just find them and follow them.

Exercise 102: Self-pleasure with a partner

Masturbation is also a wonderful liberatory practice to bring into partner sex. Self-pleasuring together, we are claiming and practicing an autonomous sexuality. We control how and when we are touched. We have more choice about the arousal level we want to explore, and our access to orgasm. We might combine self-pleasuring with partner touch, or enjoy caring erotic connection by simply witnessing each other self-pleasure.

Exercise 103: Erotic massage

I have written a whole book on *Erotic Massage for Healing and Pleasure.* There are many considerations and techniques that I cover in that book, but what is most important in the context of *Science for Sexual Happiness* is that massage separates giving and receiving.

When there is no mutual giving and receiving happening simultaneously, erotic massage provides an arena in which the person receiving touch can stay safe and focused. An educated and experienced erotic massage practitioner will learn to coach the receiver's voice, so that they can direct all touch. It is healing to practice asking for what we want while we are receiving erotic touch. It is healing to feel loving attention focused on our whole bodies, integrating and awakening the genitals and anus—these parts that are so often ignored and shamed. In the way I teach erotic massage, the person receiving is encouraged to breathe into body sensation and decide, moment to moment, what their body wants. Slowing down gives time to notice physical sensations, and also notice what is going on for us emotionally. We may notice feelings of numbness. We may notice that consciously or unconsciously we have been rushing ourselves to be 'ready' for penetrative sex. We may touch hidden sexual wounds. A massage done slowly and with great care can be deeply healing. It can bring tears of relief, joy or grief.

Helen came to my practice with the intention of healing. She was sexually abused as a child and violently assaulted as a young woman. In her fifties, she was cut off from sexual pleasure. "When my genitals are touched I feel either numbness—or pain," she told me during the intake process. Helen came for sessions every other week for over a year. The healing she experienced involved scar tissue remediation. She also needed to experience her efficacy and power in sexual situations, and to practice having voice and choice. In the learning environment provided by erotic massage, she was able to feel into her body's capacity for sensation and bring her genitals to life.

As a person offering erotic massage to someone reclaiming erotic pleasure, you need to stay in communication. Be sensitive to non-verbal cues. If you feel the person on the table flinch, become restless, or stop moving—if you see that their breathing has become shallow, their brow furrowed, or their facial expression flat—if they are struggling for words or their voice goes high—these are important clues that they are having a fight, flight, appease, freeze or dissociate reaction. Stop! Be still and allow the person receiving to come back into their bodies, and back into connection with you. Receiving erotic touch can raise entangled memories and complex emotions.

As survivors of trauma and neglect, we need to learn, very slowly, to accept sexual touch, communicate desire, and stay present to waves and floods of deep feeling. Erotic massage can provide a safe container of one-way touch in which we can overcome habits of dissociation and work through the trauma embedded in our bodies.

I am a passionate advocate of erotic massage, because I have witnessed many miracles emerging through erotic bodywork. When offered with appropriate safeguards and clear boundaries, erotic massage allows us to access sexual energy at our own pace. We can learn to feel erotic energy fully and freely, and in this learning, find our way home.

Exercises 104–105: Erotic ritual

Erotic rituals, such as those shown on the Orgasmic Yoga website, or offered through the OneTaste community, can be beautiful and useful practices for people who want to explore sex outside the box. It is vital that all participants understand that for the ritual to be beneficial, it needs to be offered in a safe container. It is important to have clarity about time allowed for the ritual, and expectations of the partners. As survivors of trauma or neglect who are reclaiming erotic pleasure, we are very vulnerable. It is so important to have clear boundaries and roles, and stick to them, despite pressure you are likely to feel to proceed from a ritual exchange to a more conventional interactive erotic exchange. If we can find a partner or friend with whom to practice this ritual approach to erotic touch, it can offer a profound experience of sinking into awareness of physical, emotional, mental and spiritual dimensions of erotic sensation.

The basic practice is setting time and space aside for an erotic ritual. The particular ritual described below focuses on genital touch rather than whole-body touch. It is a way of experiencing genital sensation in a context that is different from erotic interactions and masturbation habits. It is a mindfulness meditation rather than foreplay. Orgasm is not a goal or an end (if it happens, enjoy!). People who do this ritual repeatedly over several weeks or months can find their capacity for genital feeling hugely expand, along with their sense of vitality and confidence.

The giver of touch stays clothed while the receiver of touch removes clothes from the waist down, and lies down on a bed or the floor with legs open. The giver sits comfortably beside the receiver. When the receiver of touch is ready, the giver rests a hand for some moments in the genital area. They then apply lube and stroke the receiver's genitals for fifteen minutes, using a timer. Repeating the same stroke over and over helps change this into a ritual rather than a regular erotic experience. Keep checking that the person receiving touch is not going into 'enduring' or 'appease' mode. Keep asking for guidance, affirming your willingness to change. Say thank you whenever you receive a correction or guidance.

Variation: Do this as a self-pleasuring ritual.

Erotic ritual for people with vulvas

The giver rests a hand for some moments on the receiver's genital area.

Then apply lube and stroke the receiver's genitals for fifteen minutes, using a timer.

Try a repetitive stroke such as this:

1. Pet downwards, using your three longest fingers. The middle finger glides along the shaft and glans of the clitoris and the outside of the vaginal opening, the other two fingers run along the place where the thigh meets the labia. As a variation, try running your outside fingers between the inner and outer labia.

2. Make a Y with forefinger and index finger and stimulate the clitoris and the labia with a scissoring motion.

3. Massage the glans through the hood of the clitoris, or pull back the hood and massage the glans very, very lightly and very, very slowly.

Remember to use lots and lots of lube. Silicone lube may be best for this practice.

Have the receiver guide the touch, going for what is pleasurable without judging arousal or the absence of arousal. This is a meditation, so just experience the physical and emotional sensations. End with the giver quietly holding the receiver's genitals, with complete attention.

After getting dressed, share a description of one particularly memorable moment of sensation while avoiding evaluating or comparing the experience.

Erotic ritual for people with penises

The giver rests a hand for some moments on the receiver's genital area.

Then apply lube and stroke the receiver's genitals for fifteen minutes, using a timer.

Try a repetitive stroke such as this:

1. Hold the penis at the base with one hand, and then massage the frenulum and the glans with your flat palm, gliding over the head of the penis and the belly.

2. Grasp the shaft of the penis and glide your fist down over the shaft and glans.

3. Massage the glans and coronal ridge by grasping the penis and twisting off with a spiraling motion.

Have the receiver guide the touch, going for what is pleasurable without judging hard or soft, arousal or the absence of arousal. This is a meditation, so just experience the physical and emotional sensations. End with the giver quietly holding the receiver's genitals, with complete attention.

After getting dressed, share a description of one particularly memorable moment of sensation while avoiding evaluating or comparing the experience.

Exercise 106: Play with toys

There are so many wonderful sex toys. There are vibrators that can offer otherwise anorgasmic women access to multiple orgasms and wonderful pleasures. Dildos can eliminate any worries men have over not getting hard, or being too big or too small. Prostate stimulators and butt plugs can open up anal pleasures and contribute to pelvic floor health. Silicone dolls can offer comfort and companionship along with erotic stimulation. Be playful and open about bringing toys into your life and integrating them into self-pleasuring and partner play.

Lose the orgasm container

Orgasms are lovely sometimes, but chasing an orgasm puts unnecessary pressure on self-pleasuring or partner play. Pursuing an orgasm can make sex into a goal-oriented activity. People too often have sex in an orgasm container, so that as soon as those involved have an orgasm, they are done. What about using a time container instead? If you have an hour for sexual activity, you can enjoy whatever unfolds within that hour. It may include one or more orgasms, or it may include other joys. We also need to lose the idea that people 'give' (or fail to 'give') each other orgasms. Let each person take responsibility for their own pleasure, guiding their partners, and integrating self-touch. Sometimes our pleasure may include one or many orgasms. Sometimes what matters more is simply enjoying the journey without a destination, feeling what is, and staying present with all that unfolds within and around us while we engage in erotic play.

Dealing with genital pain

In my experience of working with survivors of sexual trauma and neglect, genital pain can often complicate efforts to reconnect with erotic pleasures. Genital pain can result from many factors including a chronic pelvic clench, scar tissue from trauma, and the atrophy of genital tissues from the absence of blood flow in neglected areas. Be sure to confer with your doctor and ask for a referral to a pelvic pain specialist. Effective treatment for genital pain includes therapy that helps us become aware of our chronic pelvic clench and to release it. Specialized physiotherapy using biofeedback techniques can be helpful. Mindfulness practices such as those described throughout this book help calm our neurology so we can feel less distress around the pain. Changing our habitual thinking about sex is also helpful in calming our nervous system and developing a larger repertoire of pleasurable practices. Genital massage is another way to gently heal genital pain, address adhesions from scar tissue and encourage blood flow in affected areas. I have described techniques for 'Healing Painful Sex' in my book *Erotic Massage* and teach them at my workshop 'Pelvic Pain Clinic.' Whatever you do, do not force penetration and retraumatize your genitals!

SEXUAL PARTNERS OUTSIDE THE BOX

In the chapter on attachment we explored the importance of caring relationships. We have a profound biophysical need for safety and belonging. Our nervous system is wired through love and connection. And we have very limited ideas about how our needs can be met. Creating new sexual culture can involve expanding possibilities in this realm.

Erotic friendship

Erotic friendship is one way I have enjoyed exploring expanded possibility. Can we add erotic play into a caring connection with others? There may be people in our life or community whom we wouldn't pick as either romantic or sexual partners, but who can become beloved playmates in a co-created journey of discovery.

Erotic community

Exploring erotic energy in a group is a rich and multifaceted experience that feels to me like a crucial part of the sexual healing we need as individuals and as a society. We find support for our own unique journeys, while we resonate with shared commonalities. Communal erotic practice is part of many ancient and indigenous human cultures.

In addition, we can think outside the box and build erotic community with many people.

Workshops such as those offered by somatic sex educators and the Body Electric School are great places to begin building an erotic community.

Professional erotic service providers

The exchange of money for intimacy is widely denigrated, and even (in some forms) prohibited and criminalized in this culture. Why is 'the oldest profession' subject to such scorn? It is true that sex work can be a desperate choice by marginalized people who are injured and endangered by the thousand ways sex work is despised. But for people who are reconnecting with sex in the wake of trauma and neglect, working with professional erotic service providers can be an important part of the journey. Working with a professional, we can engage with the erotic at our own pace in a relationship of our own choosing. In my own personal healing journey, I needed the safe container that was provided by working with professional intimacy educators who offered erotic touch in a clearly boundaried container. Paid professional exchanges were a safe place for me to explore and learn to be attuned to my own body while experiencing erotic touch.

Long-term relationships

A long-term relationship is often the last place people go to learn to explore and express themselves erotically. Long-term relationships can be places where survivors of trauma and neglect hide out and avoid sex. When one or both partners want to reclaim erotic pleasure, relationships are challenged and transformed.

Sadly, it can feel easier to change partners than to change established patterns with an existing partner. In long-term relationships, sex becomes something people make happen rather than something that happens to us. We don't have the hormonal surges that can make sex in new relationships feel paramount and effortless. There is a widely- held cultural myth that for sex to be great we need to be swept away by desire. Perhaps especially for survivors of trauma and neglect, it can feel very uncomfortable to choose sex consciously, deliberately and mindfully. It can seem silly to schedule time for erotic interactions with a long-term partner. But if people want to come alive to their erotic potential, both individually and in relationships, they need to cultivate sexual energy. This means giving time, attention, and approval to erotic joy.

Couples get into soul-draining patterns where one person is always the initiator of sexual interactions and the other experiences sex as a demand placed upon them. I often see people in relationships devoid not only of erotic touch, but of all touch, because every touch is perceived as a demand for intercourse. Other couples feel they must wait to heal all their relationship issues before they can say yes to sex, loading erotic pleasure with a requirement for tender feelings that may be in short supply in the absence of sex. I suggest people experiment with expressing a range of emotions sexually: anger, frolic, naughtiness, and mindlessness. Play doctor, play dominatrix, have sex in a car, have a wild affair with your spouse.

When long-term couples choose to explore the path of pleasure, learning and conscious sexuality, an astonishing richness becomes possible. We can share profound bonding, ecstatic awareness, and infinite variety within a single relationship.

Dimensions of sexual experience

People get caught up in conflicts and shaming around the go-to ways they play in the different dimensions of sexual experience. We all have our go-to ways of being sexual. But when we are unconscious in our choice of sexual scripts, or we think our way is the only 'right' way, we come into unnecessary conflict with one another.

Psychologist Donald Mosher was the first to name three different scripts people have for sexual experience: Partner Engagement, Erotic Trance, and Role Play. For each sexual script, there are learnings and competencies that can help us go deeper.

Partner engagement

For people whose go-to script is partner engagement, sex is primarily an opportunity for profound relationship with another person. You want lots of interaction, eye gazing, cuddling, and connected touch. You love the emotions that flow through mind and body with sexual touch and the mutual giving and receiving of pleasure. You want to be sexual with a partner who is special and unique. Sex is an expression of love. Great sex might mean an archetypal, mystical union and a merging with the divine in your beloved.

Erotic trance

For people whose primary sexual script is erotic trance, sex is an opportunity for a profound experience of thrilling body sensation. You might tend to close your eyes to better concentrate on what is unfolding within. You are likely to feel pleasure most readily with a non-intrusive partner. Great sex in this style is an immersion in sensation that can be transporting, even hallucinatory—an ecstatic union with all life.

Role play

People whose go-to script is role play really enjoy the erotic imagination, and the way thoughts can stimulate the nervous system to trigger arousal and orgasm. This is a script couples often explore unconsciously, with power dynamics in relationships, or secretly, with unshared fantasies. If people can create an environment of permission and playfulness around exploring role play, they can have a lot of fun.

All three dimensions of sexual experience are immensely valuable. Each has its wondrous gifts. Yet all too often we meet each other at the lowest common denominator. Someone whose go-to script is erotic trance will grudgingly offer a partner a few words of love, then hurriedly go back into their inner focus. Someone whose go-to script is partner engagement will complain they are always unloved and unmet. Fantasies stay as underdeveloped snippets of erotic thoughts. Role play is explored in unconscious habits of anger and dependency. We can choose instead to celebrate all the ways the erotic shows up in our partners and ourselves. If we get through our initial discomfort, we can dive deeply into each sexual script. When we commit to learning and playing with conscious awareness in multiple dimensions of sexual experience, we bring new joy into our lives and relationships.

Sex and Spirit

Many ancient and indigenous cultures honor sexual energy as sacred. In Western culture, for many centuries, sex and spirit have been characterized as opposite forces by institutions that aim to control and ration spiritual experiences. Many of us unconsciously internalize this idea, and imagine that sex is something lower and spirit something higher, or that sex is physical while spirit is ethereal. We can reclaim erotic pleasure from this separation, and explore the sacred prayer of our own bodies. Our physical and emotional experiences of erotic pleasure can guide us to know spirit through our cells.

Sex can offer an unparalleled experience of joy and integration. There is a sense of wholeness that comes through merging ecstatic body pleasures with loving human connection. Caring erotic exchanges with ourselves and others can generate embodied experiences of linking soul and universe in our genitals. Erotic pleasure can be a way to access altered states and other worlds. Beyond ordinary reality and everyday consciousness, we can connect with a deep, trans-personal wisdom that can guide our lives.

Despite a personal history of trauma and neglect, and a dearth of romantic partners, I have been able to cultivate the experience of sexual ecstasy. I am regularly held in the unity of bodysoul, open-hearted love and unfolding mystery. Many people have transcendent sexual experiences once in a lifetime, or early in an erotic relationship. But I know they need not be so rare. Through the erotic we have a *techne* of profound joy—an art and craft through which we can directly apprehend, breathe, embody and share a numinous reality where we feel at one, at peace, and fully alive.

Learning to practice this *techne* of joy involves building our inner capacities. Integrating various parts of the brain, and brain with body, and brain and body with language and imagination. We can weave together words and sensations, feelings and thoughts. As we become more courageous and caring, we are integrating spirit and emotions. We build trust in our ability to feel fully and deeply, in both the realm of contentment and the realm of excitement.

We need to keep ourselves safe while challenging ourselves enough to gradually build the capacity for expanded ecstatic states. We are wired for ecstatic embodiment, through the neurotransmitters that convey euphoria and bliss between brain cells and body tissues, and in the convergence of thousands of nerve endings in our genitals. However, when we don't have a foundational sense of safety, our cells are chronically bathed in stress hormones and neurochemicals that actively obstruct pleasure, learning, happiness, connection and ecstatic sexual response.

On my personal journey of reclaiming erotic pleasure, I have come a long way, and I trust I will continue unfolding what is possible for the rest of my life. Each year I find my way to more physical and emotional pleasure, even though I am also still learning to release held pain, shame, habitual numbness, and my chronically cramped pelvic floor. I am learning to stay increasingly present to my body's capacity for sexual feeling without needing to judge it, stifle it, or make a story out of it. I am learning how to separate my erotic responses from sticky attachments to one person or situation. Through joyful and empowering body experiences, I am integrating the knowledge I need in order to make more life-affirming choices about sex.

Learning to practice the *techne* of joy also involves building a world of relationships that can hold this. Changes in culture and community come slowly, but they can begin within ourselves, as we learn to wield power for goodness, engage in productive conflict, and live a commitment to loving connection.

Learning to practice the *techne* of joy also involves building erotic relationships with nature and spirit. In my personal embodied experience, and in the paradigm of 'sacred intimacy' that informs me, sex is holy. Erotic energy is life force energy. It is an aspect of constellations, trees and tides. Sexual ecstasy is a way to honor and practice the divine in ourselves and others. It is a way to pray, celebrate, heal and transform the human relationship with nature and spirit. With every cell in our bodies, we can be and become love.

Exercise 107: Erotic spirit mandala

Use the image on the following page to create a mandala about your personal intersection of sex and spirit. Are there ancestors, objects, practices, and possibilities that guide and inspire you? Where and what is erotic and how does that resonate with your soul? Do you have memories, imagination, caring connections, communities, books, dreams or desires that evoke an intersection of sex and spirit? Use colors, words and doodles to imagine what erotic spirit means to you.

Bibliography

Allione, Tsultrim. *Feeding Your Demons: Ancient Wisdom for Resolving Inner Conflict.* Little, Brown and Company, 2008.

Badenoch, Bonnie. *Being a Brain-Wise Therapist: A Practical Guide to Interpersonal Neurobiology (Norton Series on Interpersonal Neurobiology).* New York: W. W. Norton & Company, 2008.

Bornstein, Kate. *My Gender Workbook.* New York: Routledge, 1998.

Bornstein, Kate, and Sara Quin. *Hello Cruel World: 101 Alternatives to Suicide for Teens, Freaks and Other Outlaws.* New York: Seven Stories Press, 2006.

Bradford, Andrea, and Cindy M. Meston. 'The Impact of Anxiety on Sexual Arousal in Women.' *Behaviour research and therapy* 44.8 (2006): 1067–1077. *PubMed Central.* Web.

Buczynski, Ruth. 'NICABM - Mindfulness, Spirituality in Healing, Trauma Therapy Training, and Brain Science.' N.p., n.d. Web. 17 Apr. 2016.

Calais-Germain, Blandine. *The Female Pelvis Anatomy & Exercises.* Seattle, WA: Eastland Press, 2003.

Carter, C Sue, and Stephen W Porges. 'The Biochemistry of Love: An Oxytocin Hypothesis.' *EMBO Reports* 14.1 (2013): 12–16. *PubMed Central.* Web.

Crenshaw, Theresa L. *The Alchemy of Love and Lust.* New York, NY: Gallery Books, 1997.

Das, Anirudda. 'Masturbation in the United States,' *Journal of Sex and Marital Therapy*, (2007) 33:301.

Doidge, Norman. *The Brain's Way of Healing.* New York: Penguin, 2015.

Finkelhor, D., Hotaling, G., Lewis, I. A., & Smith, C. (1990). Sexual abuse in a national survey of adult men and women: Prevalence, characteristics and risk factors. Child Abuse & Neglect 14, 19-28. doi:10.1016/0145-2134(90)90077-7.

Fine, Cordelia. *Delusions of Gender: The Real Science Behind Sex Differences.* Icon Books Ltd, 2005.

Fraley, R. Chris. 'A Brief Overview of Adult Attachment Theory and Research.' N.p., n.d. Web. 17 Apr. 2016.

Franklin, Eric. *Pelvic Power: Mind/Body Exercises for Strength, Flexibility, Posture, and Balance for Men and Women.* Highstown, NJ: Elysian Editions, 2003.

Goldstein, Irwin et al. *Women's Sexual Function and Dysfunction: Study, Diagnosis and Treatment.* CRC Press, 2005.

Hanna, Thomas. *Somatics: Reawakening the Mind's Control of Movement, Flexibility, and Health.* Cambridge, MA: Da Capo Press Inc, 2004.

Hanson, Rick. 'Dr. Rick Hanson.' *Dr. Rick Hanson.* N.p., n.d. Web. 19 Apr. 2016.

---. *Hardwiring Happiness: The New Brain Science of Contentment, Calm, and Confidence.* New York: Harmony, 2013.

Hatfield, Robert. 'Touch and Human Sexuality.' In *Human Sexuality: An Encyclopedia.* Ed. V. Bullough, B. Bullough and A. Stein. New York: Garland Publishing, 1994.

Heller, Diane Poole. 'Thanksgiving video message from Diane.' Web http://dianepooleheller.com/thanksgiving-video-message-from-diane/ September 8, 2016.

Hendricks, Gay. *Conscious Breathing: Breathwork for Health, Stress Release, and Personal Mastery*. Bantam, 2010.

Jesse, Caffyn. *Erotic Massage for Healing and Pleasure: Plus Orgasm Coaching, Genital Anatomy, Scar Tissue Healing and More from a Pioneering Somatic Sex Educator*. erospirit, 2015.

---. *Orientation: Mapping Queer Meanings*. erospirit, 2015.

Jung, Carl G., and Carl Kerényi. *Essays on a Science of Mythology*. Trans. trans. R.F.C. Hull. Princeton: Princeton University Press, 1949. Bollingen Series XXII.

Kabat-Zinn, Jon and Thich Nhat Hanh. *Full Catastrophe Living (Revised Edition): Using the Wisdom of Your Body and Mind to Face Stress, Pain, and Illness:* Random House, 1990.

Komisaruk, Barry R., Carlos Beyer-Flores, and Beverly Whipple. *The Science of Orgasm*. Baltimore: Johns Hopkins University Press, 2006.

Lanius, Ulrich F., Sandra L. Paulsen, and Frank M. Corrigan. *Neurobiology and Treatment of Traumatic Dissociation: Towards an Embodied Self.* New York: Springer Publishing Company, 2014.

Levine, Peter A. *Healing Trauma: A Pioneering Program for Restoring the Wisdom of Your Body*. Pap/Com edition. Boulder, Colo.; Enfield: Sounds True, 2008.

Linden, David. Touch: *The Science of Hand, Heart and Mind.* New York: Viking, 2015.

Lindgren, L., S. Rundgren, O. Winsö, et al. 'Physiological Responses to Touch Massage in Healthy Volunteers.' *Autonomic Neuroscience: Basic & Clinical* (2010). 158(1–2): 105–110

Martin, Betty. 'Betty Martin.' N.p., n.d. Web. 19 Apr. 2016.

Mate, Gabor, and Peter A. Levine. *In the Realm of Hungry Ghosts: Close Encounters with Addiction*. Berkeley, Calif: North Atlantic Books, 2010.

McCraty, Rollin, and Maria A. Zayas. 'Cardiac Coherence, Self-Regulation, Autonomic Stability, and Psychosocial Well-Being.' *Frontiers in Psychology* 5 (2014): n. pag. *PubMed Central*. Web. 17 Apr. 2016.

Meaney, M. J. 'Maternal Care, Gene Expression, and the Transmission of Individual Differences in Stress Reactivity across Generations.' *Annual Review of Neuroscience* 24 (2001): 1161–1192. *PubMed*. Web.

Meston, C. M. 'Sympathetic Nervous System Activity and Female Sexual Arousal.' *The American Journal of Cardiology* 86.2A (2000): 30F–34F.

Moore, David. *The Developing Genome: An Introduction to Behavioral Epigenetics*. Oxford: Oxford University Press, 2015. Web. 17 Apr. 2016.

Morin, Jack. *The Erotic Mind: Unlocking the Inner Sources of Passion and Fulfillment*. Reprint edition. Harper Perennial, 2012.

Mosher, Donald. (1980). 3 Dimensions of depth of involvement in human sexual-response. Journal of Sex Research 16(1):1-42. Web.

Nagowski, Emily. *Come as You Are: The Surprising New Science That Will Transform Your Sex Life*. 1 edition. New York: Simon & Schuster, 2015.

National Sexual Violence Resource Center, Factsheet: Statistics about sexual violence, http://www.nsvrc.org/publications/nsvrc-publications-fact-sheets/media-packet-statistics-about-sexual-violence

Nummenmaa, Lauri et al. "Bodily Maps of Emotions." *Proceedings of the National Academy of Sciences* 111.2 (2014): 646–651. *www.pnas.org*. Web.

Ogden, Pat, Kekuni Minton, and Clare Pain. *Trauma and the Body: A Neurobiologically Informed Approach To Clinical Practice*. New York: WW Norton, 2006.

Ogden, Pat and Janina Fisher. *Sensorimotor Psychotherapy: Interventions for Trauma and Attachment*

(Norton Series on Interpersonal Neurobiology). New York: W. W. Norton & Company, 2015.

Porges, Stephen W. *The Polyvagal Theory: Neurophysiological Foundations of Emotions, Attachment, Communication, and Self-Regulation*. New York: W. W. Norton & Company, 2011.

Porter, Lauren Lindsey. 'The Science of Attachment: The Biological Roots of Love - The Natural Child Project.' N.p., n.d. Web. 17 Apr. 2016.

Roberts, Alice. *The Incredible Unlikeliness of Being: Evolution and the Making of Us.* New York: Heron Books, 2014.

Scepkowski, Lisa A., , Michaela, and Pfaus, James G. 'Neuroendocrine Factors in Sexual Desire and Motivation.' *Women's Sexual Function and Dysfunction*. CRC Press, 2005. 159–167. crcnetbase.com (Atypon). Web. 17 Apr. 2016.

Schore, Allan. 'Attachment and Regulation of the Right Brain.' *Attachment and Human Development* 2.1 (2000): 23–47.

Siegel, Daniel J. *Mindsight: The New Science of Personal Transformation*. Reprint edition. Bantam, 2010.

---. *The Mindful Brain.* New York: W. W. Norton & Company, 2007. Web. 17 Apr. 2016.

Sorrells, Morris L., James L. Snyder, Mark D. Reiss, et al. 2007. 'Fine-Touch Thresholds in the Adult Penis.' *BJU International* 99(4): 864–869.

Strozzi-Heckler, Richard. *The Art of Somatic Coaching: Embodying Skillful Action, Wisdom, and Compassion*. Berkeley, Calif: North Atlantic Books, 2014. Web. 17 Apr. 2016.

Tewfik, Ted; Chief Editor: Arlen D Meyers. 'Vagus Nerve Anatomy: Gross Anatomy, Microscopic Anatomy, Natural Variants.' http://emedicine.medscape.com/article/1875813-overview accessed September 3, 2016.

van der Kolk, Bessel. *The Body Keeps the Score: Brain, Mind, and Body in the Healing of Trauma*. Penguin Books, 2015.

Wade, Jenny. *Transcendent Sex: When Lovemaking Opens the Veil*. New York: Gallery Books, 2004.

Yang, Claire C., and Xiaogang Jiang. "Clinical Autonomic Neurophysiology and the Male Sexual Response: An Overview." *The Journal of Sexual Medicine* 6 Suppl 3 (2009): 221–228. *PubMed*.

Made in the USA
Coppell, TX
08 January 2025

44149526R00106